"It is sometimes tougher to fight my superiors than the French."

HEINZ GUDERIAN

This series deals with the history of the *Panzerwaffe* from the first German tanks in World War I to the end of World War II. The book you are holding covers the new equipment introduced and the new *Panzer Divisions* formed after the end of the Polish campaign and takes the story up to the Fall of France. Unlike the first volume, this one is by a single author who has a long-standing interest in this period.

His detailed text is accompanied by many photographs, and once again we have tried to include as many interesting previously unpublished images as possible. It is worth pointing out that most of these photographs are the work of the soldiers themselves. This means that they are not all perfectly posed, nor in exact focus, though in many cases the results are as good as those from the professional photographers of the Propaganda Companies that accompanied them on campaign.

Once again, special thanks to Thomas Jentz and Hilary Louis Doyle of *Panzer Tracts* for their help in providing the scale plans that have been used as a basis for the colour plates. Readers wanting more technical details will find the *Panzer Tracts* books essential, and more general information about some of the German tanks described here can be found in Ian Allan's separate series of books about tanks.

John Prigent
Series Editor

Publisher's Note:
The maps and two images in this volume are taken from *'Über Schlachtfelder vorwärts! – Mit dem siegreichen Heer durch Frankreich 1940'* (Ed.: Obstlt. Univ-Prof. Dr. Kurt Hesse, Leader of *Gruppe V* (Heer), *Abteilung Wehrmachtpropaganda im Oberkommando der Wehrmacht*), Wilehlm Limpert-Verlag, Berlin SW 68, 1940.

Introduction

Left and below: These Pz II Ausf C of 2 PzDiv were photographed in Germany being prepared for the eventual invasion of France. They show the uparmoured turret and hull fronts and squared-off armour added over the original rounded bows for this version. They still carry their tactical numbers on rhomboid plates, are camouflaged in grey and brown and have wide-armed white outline crosses filled in with black, but display other interesting variations in their markings as well. The two yellow dots of the division emblem seem to be carried on sides, front and rear by all of them but some also carry their company numbers in white beside white rhomboids on their superstructure rears; 621 also has these beside its driver's visor, apparently in red. All of them show other symbols on their turret rears, most of them also on their turret sides. These appear to be descendants, devised by the regiment, of the pre-war tactical symbols that identified companies and platoons, but their exact significance and their colours are no longer known.

HISTORY records few military campaigns as decisive as that of the defeat of France and the Low Countries in May and June 1940. In less than six weeks Germany had not only vanquished one of the world's great powers, it had also seemingly brought Great Britain to the point whereby it could either seek salvation through humiliating peace terms or face the prospect of invasion. When viewed all of apiece there is the perception that here was a most remarkable operation, conjured up by men of vision and executed by numerically and technically superior German armed forces against enemies whose military culture was steeped in the past. No wonder it unfolded with such precision. It was inevitable.

The great paradox of the German campaign against France and the Low Countries was that it was anything but fitting this description. Far from being certain of success, the bulk of the German High Command saw the operation as proceeding on a wing and a prayer. It was an unwarranted gamble that placed Germany's very existence on the line. It was an all or nothing affair that would either end in victory or lose Germany the war. If there was optimism aplenty when the German offensive in the West opened, it lay not with them but with the western Allies who were certain that victory would be theirs. It is therefore a most remarkable feature of this campaign that within five days of its opening the French Prime Minster was telling his British counterpart that, 'we are defeated'! How was this possible? Especially as, contrary to common perception, it was the *Deutsche Wehrmacht* (German Armed Forces) that was in many areas qualitatively and numerically inferior to those it attacked. It was in short, a synthesis of guile, imagination and, above all, the application of a way of waging war based upon combined arms, speed and audacity against an enemy whose own ideas about doing so were rooted in those of a previous generation. Above all, the German victory turned on the willingness of a few senior officers from the *Panzerwaffe*, operating at Corps level in the field, to disobey their more conservative minded superiors and run with their conviction that in the formations they commanded they wielded a new and revolutionary instrument which, if properly employed, would permit Germany to secure victory.

THE EVOLUTION OF *FALL GELB*

On 27 September 1939 – the same day that Warsaw surrendered – the heads of the respective branches of the *Deutsche Wehrmacht* (German Armed Forces) arrived at the new Chancellery in Berlin, whence Adolf Hitler had

Tanks, guns and vehicles were kept as clean as possible, by washing them with a hosepipe when in barracks. If a river was handy it was used instead and the washing done with buckets, as here where a Flak 36 8.8 cm is receiving attention on a river bank in Alsace.

summoned them. With the Polish war in its closing stages they expected to hear that, if no diplomatic rapprochement with France and Great Britain was forthcoming, then Germany would inevitably adopt a strategic defensive in preparation for an offensive in the West which the Army anticipated could take place no earlier than 1941. Indeed, the *Luftwaffe*, which had always viewed Great Britain, as 'the most dangerous enemy', did not anticipate possessing a bomber force that could properly assault that island nation until 1942. Nor did the *Kriegsmarine* differ much in its assessment as to its readiness to embark in offensive naval warfare against the western powers. The professional military consensus shared by those present was that Germany was simply unprepared to embark upon any strategic offensive against the west.

Some hours later, this same group left in a state of collective shock. Far from hearing the *Führer* express views that reflected their own convictions, the harangue to which Hitler had subjected them demanded that Germany attack in the west within a matter of weeks following the end of hostilities in Poland. Hitler's rationale stemmed from his belief that time was entirely on the side of the Allies. In terms of all the resources necessary to fight a war the French and the British had more, and the longer Germany waited to strike, the stronger and more powerful they would inevitably become. The judgement of the commander of the *Heer*, *Generaloberst* Walther von Brauchitsch, was that Hitler's demand was sheer 'insanity', a sentiment soon shared by many others in the Army hierarchy.

Insane or not, following this meeting *General* Franz Halder, Chief of Staff of the *Oberkommando des Heeres* (High Command of the Army – OKH for short) charged his second in command to work up a tentative plan for an offensive in late October. As such, these instructions were predicated on the assumption that the German offensive would be directed at the occupation of Luxembourg, Holland, Belgium and as much of northern France as possible. This would not only give protection for the vital Ruhr industrial region but also provide the *Luftwaffe* with airfields that would place them within bombing range of the United Kingdom. The limited aspirations of these objectives illustrate the degree to which at the time it was expected that the outcome would be little more than a re-run of the type of fighting of twenty years before. It thus presumed a replay of the Great War in all its appalling aspects but with the added 'refinement' of new weaponry that had come along since. Indeed, until the adoption of the alternative radical campaign plan in February 1940, all iterations of *Fall Gelb* (Case Yellow) were in essence refinements on this theme – that the *schwerpunkt* (point of maximum effort) of the German offensive, would be vested in Army Group B, and would be directed towards Holland, Belgium and Northern France.

This same presumption is illustrated by way of a comment Hitler made to his State Secretary, *Baron* Ernst von Weiszäcker, in which he stated that he expected this offensive might cost him 'a million men'. Even the *Führer* envisaged that any conflict with the Allied powers at this time would be no more than a re-run of the warfare he had experienced on the Western Front. Only the bitter experience of death on the massive scale that he and others had seen in the Great War could account for such a pessimistic aside as this. There is no suggestion here of anything that bore any relation at all to the 'all or nothing' offensive plan that was the ultimate key to victory in May 1940. Nor is there any hint that Hitler or the OKH saw the *Panzerwaffe* as anything other than an adjunct to the other, more conventional, arms of service despite its auspicious debut in Poland.

The German leader reiterated his views concerning the need for an immediate attack in the west in his 'Directive No: 6 for the Conduct of the War' of 9 October, stating that it would begin on 25 November and adhere to the objectives set by Halder in his original planning parameters with its limited territorial objectives. By that date, however, a post mortem on the outcome of the Polish campaign had revealed the degree to which the rapidity of the victory over Poland had served to disguise the dire logistic situation existing within the *Heer* and the *Luftwaffe*. *General* Wagner, the chief supply officer of the Army, stated that the war economy was in a critical state. Not only was there a shortage in the holdings of strategic metals for the armaments industries, extant ammunition stocks were only enough to service the needs of one third of the divisions earmarked for the offensive in the west, and these were only sufficient for two weeks combat. Furthermore *General* von Schell, the officer charged with oversight of the motor industry, detailed how losses in the new Panzer Divisions (see section on 'the Panzers' for details) had been far from negligible. It would also take some months to repair the many damaged machines. Of greater significance, very few of the 'heavy' *Panzer* III and *Panzer* IV models would be available for an early offensive. The *Luftwaffe* also stated that operations in Poland had proven costly with some 30 per cent of all aircraft committed either written off or seriously damaged and in need of repair. Its bomb stocks were seriously depleted and could not be replenished rapidly. Put quite simply, the *Wehrmacht* was in no state to execute the demands of its commander, nor was the economy in a position to provide the armed forces with the means to conduct the expected war of attrition that would ensue thereafter. Nonetheless, on 10 October, Hitler presented Brauchitsch and Halder with a very detailed memorandum detailing why it was still important to go ahead with this early offensive notwithstanding these logistic problems. In his conclusion, Hitler offered one highly significant concession: the timing of the offensive would depend on the readiness for combined armour-air operations such as those that had been successful in Poland.

Even though this proviso could not be met by this date, on 22 October, Hitler nonetheless brought forward the date of the offensive to 12 November. Although the Army leadership attempted to get him to change his mind, he refused. A tour by Brauchitsch and Halder of the Western Front at the beginning of November to consult with the commanders of the three army groups, who would oversee the offensive, produced a wholly negative consensus. They were all of one mind that their forces could not possibly be ready by mid-November. In particular, this view was forcibly reinforced by General Erich von Manstein, who was serving as Chief of Staff to *Generaloberst* Gerd von Rundstedt's Army Group 'A'. This officer was listened to by virtue of the fact that he had already acquired a reputation as a strategist – albeit thought by many to be arrogant and ambitious, a view certainly shared by Halder. Manstein stated emphatically that Hitler's plan would fail, in consequence of which he would soon offer up his own ideas on an alternative invasion plan that would, before long, set the 'radical cat among the conservative pigeons'. The pessimism that the two men had encountered is reflected in Halder's diary entry for 3 November. He wrote that *'none of the headquarters think that the offensive …has any prospect of success'*.

However, Halder's use of the term 'success' had nothing whatsoever to do with the expectation of securing a *decisive* victory over the French and British. Rather it was an expression of a conviction shared with his fellow senior commanders that the offensive as planned would not realise even those limited objectives set for it. This pessimism was, however, also motivated by something deeper, something more fundamental. Mediated as it was through the prism of their experiences in the Great War, it had become almost an article of faith in the upper echelons of the German military that victory over its enemies through a short war against opponents of superior strength was not possible. Small wonder that Halder at this stage baulked at the prospect of a western campaign, as little could be hoped for but a re-run of 1914-18 with an outcome that would in all probability be the same.

Nor had the Army hierarchy viewed the outcome of the Polish campaign as in any sense providing a break with the past and offering a way out of this intellectual impasse. The term 'Blitzkrieg' was an American invention, a verbal construction coined by a correspondent of Time magazine that had no counterpart in the German military lexicon, the concept being viewed with derision if it registered at all. On one thing the Army hierarchy was agreed, the Polish campaign was no exemplar for the forthcoming campaign in the west. The Polish Army was not the French Army, the latter being a far more powerful instrument and one still held at this time in great respect. Notwithstanding the pointers to the possible future conduct of warfare provided by the use of armour in Poland, Ritter von Leeb, the commander of Army Group C for the western campaign, articulated what was the prevailing mindset among the conservatively minded *Feldherren*.

'Surprise is not possible. Our sacrifices in blood will be tremendous, and we will not be able to defeat the French. An attack against France can never be launched like an attack against Poland; instead it will be protracted, and we will have extremely heavy losses'.

That senior Army commanders were unable (and perhaps unwilling) to think outside of this particular 'box' accounts for Hitler's growing frustration with them, although he was not in a position to proffer any

Continues on page 8.

This is a view through the commander's hatch of a Pz I showing how cramped it was inside the turret. The two machine gun breeches are either side of the gunsight, whose shaped rubber browpad was very necessary when it was moving across country. The browpad is offset to the left of the telescopic sight so that the commander could use his right eye for sighting.

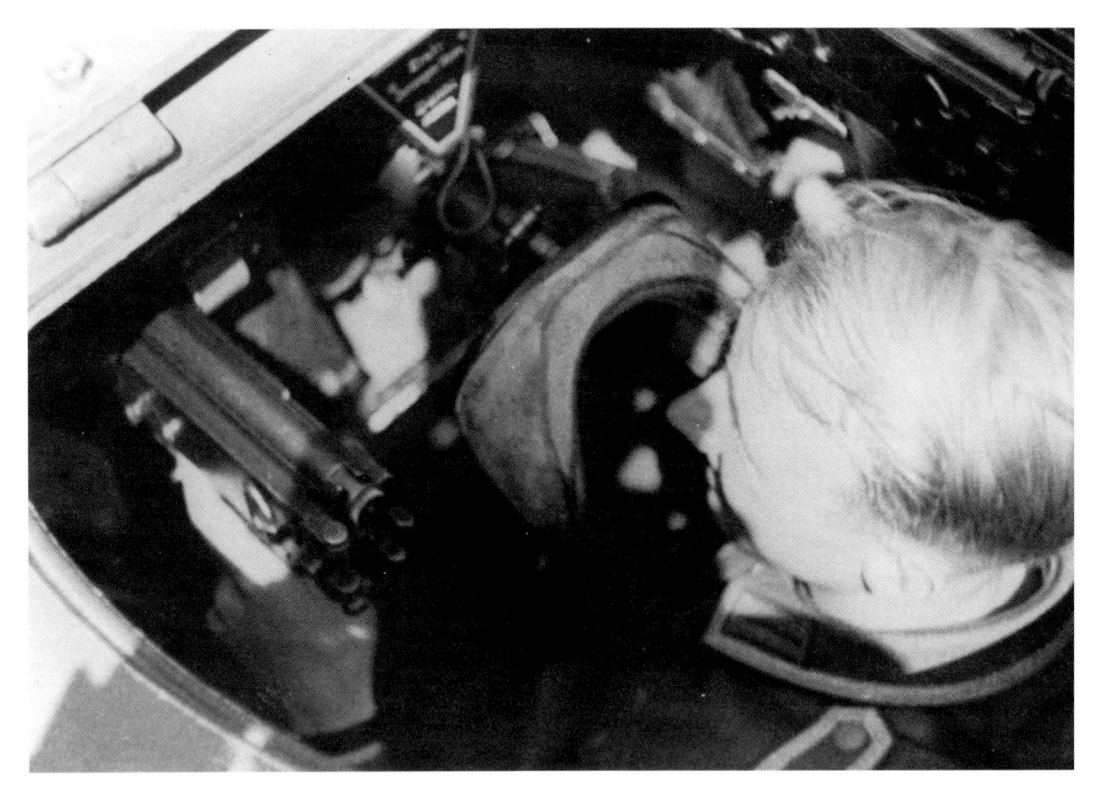

German heavy artillery was excellent. Here a Schwere 10cm Kannone 18 (s 10 cm K18 for short, meaning 'heavy 10 cm gun') is seen at Posen in Germany on 3 April 1940, limbered up and ready for the invasion. This was the German army's standard medium artillery piece, with a range of just over 18 kilometres.

INTRODUCTION 7

These 10 cm K18s photographed at Posen on 15 May 1940 prove that not all equipment was repainted in the grey and brown scheme.

This 'bunkerknacker' 8.8 cm is being towed by an unarmoured half-track; several of the special armoured tractors were knocked out in France and would have been replaced by the 'ordinary' half-track, but is impossible to be sure whether this photograph dates from that time or was taken during training for the invasion.

alternative. Having stated repeatedly that in his opinion the French would collapse quickly, he frequently gave vent to his frustration that he sensed his enemies were not across the border but among his own military. Hitler saw the army's hierarchy as members of a reactionary, conservative clique, whom he despised but nonetheless needed. He frequently spoke of 'the Zossen spirit' – his synonym for the 'defeatist' mentality that he believed pervaded the upper echelons of the Army headquarters. Nor was he oblivious to the possibility that these same 'gentlemen' might seek to move against him and mount a coup. The possibility of this was scotched when Hitler delivered his stinging rebuke to Brauchitsch on 5 November, when the commander of the Army had attempted to offer up a case for postponement of the western offensive. In a twenty minute diatribe Hitler induced in him a state of collapse. As a display of controlled intimidation it succeeded. *The Feldherren* called off their coup attempt.

This may well have been the intention behind a seemingly endless series of cancellations of the western offensive. It has been suggested that Hitler had already decided by late 1939 that a western offensive could not be launched before the spring of the following year. Thus the real purpose of the whole series of cancellations, occurring seemingly day after day through to February, was designed to keep the army leadership off balance and their attention focused exclusively on the need to constantly prepare for an imminent offensive.

When Halder presented *Aufmarschanweisung: Fall Gelb* – the first draft of 'Case Yellow', the designated codename of the offensive – on 19 October, Hitler had rounded on him claiming that what he had been presented with was little more than a rehash of the old Schlieffen Plan. He caustically commented was this 'the best they could come up with?' Hitler's comparison was correct only in the sense that the German offensive would be similarly directed through Belgium. He was in error though in invoking Schlieffen in a more profound sense, for that plan had been always been predicated on the requirement to secure a rapid and total victory over the French Army in the field. However, that of course was what the conservatively minded *Feldherren* deemed to be impossible.

Hitler's unhappiness, and his suggested modifications of the proposals, however unrealistic, were nevertheless incorporated by Halder into a second variant of the plan which he presented ten days later. Characterised by a dispersion of effort – one of the key heresies in German military thinking – it proposed not only retaining the main attack through Belgium but also envisaged secondary attacks further south along the line Liege–Namur. Nor was the *Führer* enthused by this proposal. In this, he was not alone. The solution to the impasse, when it came, was a plan addressed at securing that very thing thought impossible – absolute victory in the field. However so radical were its assumptions, and so audacious its proposed execution, that it was regarded as little short of fantasy.

ENTER VON MANSTEIN

As Chief of Staff to von Rundstedt's Army Group A, Lt. General Erich von Manstein was party to the contents of the initial plan for *Gelb* quite early on. He was not impressed. Although it took a few weeks for an alternative to gestate in his mind, when it did emerge it seemed to proffer a genuine substitute. However, the problem lay in the twin assumptions that underpinned it.

Firstly, it required the *schwerpunkt* of the German offensive to be shifted from Army Group B to Army Group A. The primary thrust of the offensive would now be directed through the Ardennes at the town of Sedan on the River Meuse. Following the crossing of this river obstacle German armour would then push very rapidly westward, without awaiting the arrival of the follow–up infantry, to the Channel coast of France thereby cutting off all Allied forces in Belgium. Herein lay the second, and for the likes of von Brauchitsch and Halder the most radical and unacceptable, dimension to his proposal. Given the degree to which the plan was predicated on the need for speed, the main drive both through the Ardennes and thereafter to the Channel would have to be executed by the *SchnellTruppen* – the Panzer Divisions.

Inasmuch as von Manstein had, at that time, no practical experience in the operation of a Panzer formation, his plan is remarkable in the degree to which he believed such a new arm of service could be allotted the primary role in so risky an enterprise. However, his thinking had not been carried out in isolation. It so happened that General Heinz Guderian, commander of XIX. *Panzerkorps*, was billeted in a hotel in close proximity to Manstein's own in Koblenz. As the foremost proponent in the German Army for the primacy of the role of the tank arm in the *Heer*, Guderian had been highly influential in (albeit not exclusively responsible for) the evolution of the *SchnellTruppen* thus far. He had seen Poland as but a partial testing ground of the armour concept. Manstein's proposal, however, offered the possibility of demonstrating, on the most dramatic canvas possible, a vindication of all he had been asserting over the years about the war-winning potential of large bodies of armour.

It was Guderian who now advanced the thesis that not just some of the Panzer Divisions should be given this task, but all of them! While von Manstein was undoubtedly responsible for the strategic vision and

These photographs show details of the towed version of the 'bunkerknacker' 8.8 cm. Unlike those photographed in Czechoslovakia, they now carry the standard grey and brown camouflage. The hinged side arms of their carriages are modified from the anti-aircraft version of the gun to swing lower so that they can support them if firing from the carriages became necessary.

the author of the highly detailed planning document that emerged, it was to Guderian he turned for the specialist advice and insight that could only be gleaned from one who had actual experience of Panzer operations. These Manstein incorporated into his memorandum. Of these, the most important was the problem of risk entailed in such an extended area of open flanks generated as the Panzer Divisions plunged into northern France, en route to the Channel. The distance to be covered was about 300 kilometres, with every one potentially vulnerable to French counter-attack. Guderian countered by saying that this could be forestalled by launching counter-attacks to the south by small armoured units detached from the main body of the Panzer Divisions. These would serve to distract the French or spoil any such operations that they might intend to launch.

Manstein put forward his first memorandum of what was subsequently to be called the 'Sickle-Cut Plan' (the name was coined by Winston Churchill) on 31 October 1939, but chose not to mention Guderian's name and downplayed the pivotal role of the P*anzerwaffe*. This may have been discreet inasmuch as the mere mention of Guderian's name prompted a somewhat irate conditioned reflex in some members of the upper command echelon (on the other hand von Manstein was also not partial to sharing the limelight with others). He followed this first with a further six memoranda through to early January 1940, with each going further than the last in the audacity of its concept. On all occasions, OKH simply filed them away. It seemed to them that Manstein's ideas transgressed virtually every operational maxim of warfare held holy by the German military establishment. Furthermore, all turned on their acceptance that armour and not infantry would and could provide the cutting edge of this offensive. And so matters remained until 10 January 1940.

Although the crash of a German light plane at Mechelen in Belgium and the recovery of a copy of *Aufmarschanweisung No:2* from it by Belgian authorities (the Allies were quickly informed of its content) prompted Hitler to postpone the planned January offensive, it did not lead directly to the adoption of Manstein's alternative. In the meantime, Halder had succeeded in getting von Manstein 'kicked upstairs' when the latter was given command of an Army Corps at Stettin. The whole notion might then have died a death had it not been for the outrage of a number of von Manstein's supporters at Army Group A's headquarters. Taking advantage of a visit by Hitler's chief military aide, this little coterie of middle ranking officers who believed in Manstein's ideas briefed *Major* Schmundt as to the general content of the plan and the manner in which it seemed to have been stonewalled by OKH. Knowing that Hitler himself had expressed very general opinions about the possibility of doing something at Sedan, Schmundt told Hitler about the substance of the conversation on his return to Berlin on 2 February. It was not coincidental, then, that on that same day Hitler decided to shift the *schwerpunkt* of the German offensive away from Belgium to Sedan, ordering Jodl on 13 February to instruct Halder and OKH to proceed in their planning on that assumption.

Four days later, von Manstein was invited to present his case to Hitler at the Reich Chancellery. Although they had met before (in photographs and on film von Manstein can be seen standing below Hitler when the dictator took the salute at the victory parade in Warsaw) this was probably the first time that von Manstein impinged on Hitler's consciousness and was fleshed out as a person. Notwithstanding Manstein's very competent presentation of his ideas, Hitler's view of the man is interesting: 'Certainly a bright fellow with great operational talent, but I do not trust him'. It was not a view that Hitler ever changed, even though von Manstein's star was subsequently to ascend meteorically under the *Führer*'s aegis. The upshot of this meeting was however to confirm the German leader in embracing Manstein's concept, albeit very rapidly coming to see it as his own – a position on the matter he would retain thereafter. That being said it is, however, a truism that unless Hitler had seen the potential in Manstein's proposal – the very nature of its audacity appealing to a man who always claimed to gamble on the greatest odds – and ordered that in its basic concept it be adopted, by OKH, then it would never have become the accepted basis for *Fall Gelb*. On the day after the meeting Hitler acceded to Manstein's thesis that the strongest armoured forces now be allocated to Army Group A. From here on, von Manstein was no longer involved in any of the planning that underpinned the final version of *Gelb*.

That task now fell to the Head of the OKH who, until Hitler's order of 17 January, had opposed Manstein at every turn – Franz Halder, the Chief of the German General Staff. He now embraced the concept with all of the enthusiasm of a 'Damascus Road' convert even in the face of formidable opposition from many of his colleagues who saw the plan as the road to ruin. For Halder, on reflection, Manstein's plan did have merit. Its success turned on the realisation of a number of vital objectives.

A major attack through the Ardennes Forest would restore the element of surprise. German intelligence knew that the Ardennes was *believed* by the French Army to be impassable for large numbers of tanks. However, it was absolutely vital that the Allies had no hint, until it was too late, that the true centre of gravity of the German offensive effort lay not in Belgium but to the south, through the 'impassable' Ardennes.

To ensure this, the Allies had to be duped into playing to their preconceptions. One of the fortuitous aspects of the loss of the plans for *Gelb* in January was that it precipitated a French and British assembly of their forces as if they were about to move into Belgium. What prompted this was an error in communication between Brussels and the Allies which led the latter to believe that they were being invited to move their forces into the country. What it served to do was to reveal their strategic intentions. As early as January, OKH had every reason to suppose that Allied strategy was predicated on the assumption that the main German offensive drive would come *through Belgium and nowhere else*. The assemblage of German forces and their operations on the opening days of the offensive must therefore be directed towards confirming the Allies in their rigidly held preconceptions as to German intentions.

To that end, it would not be possible to employ all the Panzer Divisions with Army Group A as Guderian desired and here Halder was correct. Although the bulk of the 10 Panzer Divisions would be allocated to Army Group A, it would be necessary to ensure that Army Group B had enough to generate, and preserve for three to five days, the illusion that the mass of German armour was committed in Belgium.

It was for this reason that the eventual weighting of armoured divisions was 3 to 7 in favour of Army Group A. However, given that the primary role of Army Group B was one of deception, the three Panzer Divisions deployed in Holland and Belgium would field far more light tanks, with the bulk of the more powerful medium *Panzer* IIIs and IVs being allocated to the three *Panzerkorps* of Army Group A.

For the same reason the bulk of the *Luftwaffe* would also be required to support Army Group B for the opening three days of the offensive. This was to reinforce the Allied perception, generated by their reading of the conduct of the German campaign in Poland, that where the Panzers were operating, there too the *Luftwaffe* would be found.

In order to ensure that the Allied forces were fully drawn into the trap, nothing would be done to hinder their advance into it. Therefore, OKH directed that the *Luftwaffe* was not to interdict Allied forces advancing into Belgium.

But one area that was to bedevil the Germans once the offensive had begun was the degree to which the armoured formations would be permitted to exercise independence of action. Halder made it clear in the final variant of *Fall Gelb* issued on 24 February that they would not be permitted to do so. Armour would still be tied to the infantry with the role of the former still to assist the latter. Originally, Halder did not envisage German forces crossing the Meuse before the eighth day of the offensive. He was persuaded to modify this so that motorised infantry formations could force crossings on the fourth day and establish bridgeheads on the west bank. These formations would then wait about four days until the infantry arrived before the advance across France begun with infantry and armour acting in concert. Although Halder would claim that he was the originator of the plan, it is clear from the contents of this document that he was still a world away from how it had been envisaged by von Manstein and Guderian.

Even in this far more conservative form, Halder's plan led to an explosion amongst the *Feldherren*, all of whom saw in it a recipe for absolute disaster. The whole edifice was, in their view, predicated on so many unlikely assumptions that it simply could not succeed. In their opposition they threw at him every contingency that spoke against its success. To his credit, and notwithstanding the degree to which he had emasculated Manstein's original idea, he argued his corner and stuck by his guns. In his seminal work 'To lose a battle' Alistair Horne cites a meeting between Fedor von Bock, the commander of Army Group A, and Halder in the latter's flat in Berlin. They were old friends and von Bock expressed himself without inhibition. His words are also representative of those of all his colleagues. He started by telling Halder he was playing with Germany's destiny:

'You will be creeping by 10 miles from the Maginot Line with the flank of your breakthrough and hoping the French will watch inertly! You are cramming the mass of the tank units together into the sparse roads of the Ardennes mountain country, as if there is no such thing as air power! And, you then hope to be able to lead an operation as far as the coast with an open southern flank 200 miles long, where stands the mass of the French Army!' Bock concluded by saying that this transcended 'the frontiers of reason'.

The French would have agreed absolutely. That is why, in the end, it never occurred to them until too late that the Germans might try something as bold, audacious and risky as Manstein's plan.

Allied strategy in May 1940

What hamstrung the ability of the French to formulate a truly effective strategy to meet a German offensive whenever it was to be launched was Belgium's continuing adherence to the neutrality it had naively declared in 1936. Prior to that date it had been in military alliance with France and its planning assumption up to that point had been, that in the event of war with Germany, the defence of France and Belgium would best be achieved by meeting the enemy on the short, but well fortified, Belgian-German border. With the outbreak of the war in September 1939, the Allies had hoped that the Belgians would see the logic of returning to the alliance and establishing a common strategy for mutual defence. The Belgians would have none of it. They clung desperately to the hope that their neutrality would save them in the inevitable coming fight between the two giants on their borders. Such hopes evaporated when the planning document for Germany's offensive in the west fell into their hands in January, for it was unambiguous in the manner in which it was based upon a German invasion of Holland and Belgium. Only then did the Belgian king give permission for tentative discussions to begin with the French and British about a common strategy. Out of this was to emerge the Dyle-Plan, or D-Plan, which formed the basis of the Allied reaction to the German invasion on 10 May.

However, much thought had already been exercised by the French and British General Staffs on the matter. In the view of General Gamelin, the Allied supreme commander, it would not be politically

Continues on page 14.

SCANDINAVIAN INTERLUDE

Exercise *Weserübung* – the German invasion of Denmark and Norway on 9 April 1940 – involved very few Panzer assets. At Hitler's insistence, the operation was overseen wholly by the OKW *(Oberkommando der Wehrmacht* – High Command of the Armed Forces) with no involvement whatsoever of the OKH.

Required by the former to provide a motorised brigade for the operation, OKH formed a scratch unit comprising, in the end, just one *PanzerAbteilung*. Designated *PanzerAbteilung z.b.V.40* (Panzer Detachment for special duties), it was mainly composed of *Panzer* Is. A smattering of *Panzer* IIs were also made available – primarily of those early variants that had not been uparmoured. With *Fall Gelb* in the offing, the Army was unwilling to supply any of the invaluable medium Pz.Kpfw IIIs or IVs to support the operation. Instead, it provided three *Neubaufahrzeuge*. These were non-standard Panzers, and classed as heavy tanks, weighing in at 36 tons. They were multi-turreted designs along the lines of the British Independent and Soviet T-28 tanks. They had not, however, entered series production and were thus in April 1940 surplus to Army combat needs, so were handed over for the Norwegian campaign. The role of the limited number of Panzers in this campaign was unambiguously that of infantry support – the terrain of Norway precluding any other. Although a small force of Pz.Kpfw I and IIs was employed in the invasion of Denmark, the majority of *PanzerAbteilung z.b.V.40* was shipped direct to Norway although it suffered the loss of five Panzers when their transport was sunk.

Throughout the short campaign most of the Panzers were operated from Oslo, although a small detachment of Pz.Kpfw 1s and IIs and a command Panzer operated in central Norway. The upshot of the involvement of the Panzers was to demonstrate that it would be possible to employ these machines in mountainous terrain albeit in a limited fashion. The Panzers were mainly confined to the use of the roads where they were sometimes halted by obstacles placed there by the enemy. The infantry, which was the primary fighting arm, found the fire support given by the Panzers very helpful, especially the 20mm of the *Panzer* II and the 75mm of the *Neubaufahrzeuge*. Although the Allies landed a number of light tanks in northern Norway to support their operations there, they did not meet any German armour.

A number of Panzers were lost in the short campaign. One of the *Neubaufahrzeuge* became bogged down, could not be recovered, and was blown up. A further two Pz.Kpfw IIs and eight Pz.KpfwIs were written-off. For the *Panzerwaffe*, the Norwegian campaign was a minor sideshow in its operations in 1940 when set against the campaign in France and the Low Countries where almost all of its assets were committed.

A Pz II Ausf A or B of PzAbt.z.b.V.40 in the invasion of Norway. The yellow unit sign is just visible beside the cross but is not quite clear enough to show which company the tank belonged to. Unfortunately, the location written on the back of the original print is illegible.

These two photographs of a Neubaufahrzeug of PzAbt.z.b.v. 40 (Panzer Battalion for Special Duties 40) were taken near Vaervaagen in southern Norway in 1940. The photographer wrote two different versions of the place name upon the negatives, incidentally proving the difficulty of transcribing partly-understood or misheard names from one language to another!

vor Varvang

Marsch nach Varwang

The PzJag I (PanzerJäger, or Tankhunter) mounted a Czech 4.7 cm anti-tank gun on the Pz I Ausf B chassis. This gun was more effective than the Germans' own 3.7 cm; putting it on to a self-propelled mount was given a high priority, and they were ready in time for the invasion of France. This one is seen in training at its home base of Wunsdorf in Germany before the beginning of the campaign. As yet it carries no markings, not even the standard cross, but its grey and brown camouflage is evident.

expedient to abandon either Holland or, especially, Belgium in the face of a German offensive in the west. Additionally, the campaign in Poland had made a profound impression on him. Poland had succumbed more quickly than had been expected and the German Army had revealed that its primary fighting strength would in future be vested in its new armoured formations supported by overwhelming air power. To Gamelin, it followed that any German offensive in the west, would also be led by their Panzer Divisions and they would employ the *Luftwaffe* in the same fashion.

It was for this reason that Gamelin dismissed the notion that the Germans would consider using the Ardennes as a conduit for these forces. Whilst he rejected the notion that this area was impassable – indeed, earlier wars had shown this not to be the case – it was only on the coastal plain of Belgium that the Germans would find terrain appropriate for the deployment of their Panzer Divisions, so as to emulate the Polish model. To Gamelin, *logic* therefore dictated that they would have to come through Belgium and that the best place for the Allies to meet them would be there, so as to block their advance.

Herein lies the thinking behind the Dyle–Plan. Adoption of this river line would permit the best-equipped of the Allied forces to advance into Belgium on news of a German offensive and adopt this defensive position. It would also have the advantage of screening the Gembloux Gap. This small industrial town stood at the centre of a narrow plain through which German armour would need to proceed if it were to attempt a wheeling manoeuvre along the lines of the Schlieffen Plan. This position had been identified in the enemy documentation captured in January as having key significance. In the final variant of the D-Plan, the northernmost point of the Allied line was extended as far as the Dutch city of Breda. Underpinning the D-Plan was the presumption that Allied forces would move rapidly into Belgium on news of the start of the German offensive and that they would be in place on the D-line *before* contact was made with the enemy.

By moving the best of their forces so far into Belgium, the weakest and therefore most poorly defended part of the Allied line was that between Namur and Sedan – the Ardennes sector. Below that was the Maginot line. In view of Gamelin's perception of the unsuitability of the Ardennes for massed German armour, it is not surprising that the sector was mainly held by weak and poorly-equipped second and third class divisions.

However, the D-Plan was clearly a case of 'putting all one's eggs in one basket'. The advance of the Allied forces into Belgium, to take up station along the D-line, would use up the best of their forces. This would leave them little in the way of quality reserves to deal with any unforeseen contingency. Herein lies its greatest weakness. So certain was Gamelin that he had divined the only possible option available to the Germans that he had made absolutely no allowance for the unexpected for, to his mind, there could be none!

At the start of the German offensive in the west, the D-Plan and its assumptions had become an article of faith of such certitude in the Allied ranks that it generated a mindset closed to the possibility that the Germans might embrace an altogether different strategy. The French were in receipt of intelligence prior to 10 May that did indeed suggest that, once the balloon went up, the D-Plan would be executed without demur and the Allies would march to their doom in Belgium like automatons.

History has rarely provided a better example to illustrate the truth of one of Sun Tzu's sayings: 'To secure ourselves from defeat lies in our hands, but the opportunity of defeating the enemy is provided by the enemy himself'.

The state of the *Panzerwaffe*: October 1939-May 1940

Although the still nascent German tank arm played a highly publicised and significant role in the defeat of Poland in September 1939, it nonetheless sustained significant losses in the process. Of the nearly 3,500 Panzers of all types available to the *Feldheer* (Field Army) and *Ersatzheer* (Reserve Army) on 1 September 1939, 2,859 were actually committed to the invasion. Of these, 236 were written-off as total losses, and many others were in need of repair.

Given that well over three quarters of the Panzers committed to *Fall Weiss* (Case White, the codename for this operation) comprised the weakly-armed and poorly-protected light *Panzers* I and II, it is not surprising that these types fared the worst with nearly 170 written-off. As a percentage of write-offs compared to numbers committed, however, the greatest loss was sustained by the small number of medium *Panzer* IIIs, with just under a third of the 87 committed by the *Feldheer* on 1 September struck from the inventory thereafter. As the type was designated to become the primary medium tank of the *Panzerwaffe*, this perhaps did not augur well. The impact of these losses was reduced by the knowledge that a number of those incurred were early models of the Pz III, which formed over a quarter of the type committed to the campaign. Nineteen *Panzer* IVs and five *Panzerbefehlswagen* (in short Pz.Bef.Wg, meaning command tank) were also total losses. Nonetheless, the performance of both the Pz III and Pz IV had been deemed successful enough for them to be accepted as the standard equipment for all tank battalions.

Even though these numbers were not drastic, the strain placed on the participating Panzer and motorised formations in *Fall Weiss* would have precluded any possibility of their involvement in any decisive fashion in the very early offensive in the west that Hitler demanded. Such had been the scale of overall losses among the tanks, prime movers and support vehicles that, according to *General* Adolf von Schell who had oversight of the motor industry, it would take until the spring of 1940 before the motorised formations were 'ready for large-scale operations after replenishing their shortages'. Furthermore, if Hitler had had his way in the matter of a 1939 offensive in the west, the qualitative gap between certain aspects of German tanks and those of the western Allies would have been even greater than it was in May 1940. An early western offensive would have seen the respective tank forces go head to head in a manner that did not occur in 1940, with an outcome that probably would have favoured the French (the point about the 1940 campaign is that during its course most German Panzers never did encounter the greater number of French tanks). The numerous cancellations of *Fall Gelb* (Case Yellow, the codename for the western campaign) were thus to benefit the *Panzerwaffe*. The tank force that eventually led the assault on France and the Low Countries was both numerically and qualitatively superior to that employed to invade Poland in September 1939.

Nonetheless, and despite the prominence given to the role of the Panzers in the Polish campaign, the building of new tanks did not go to the top of the list of priorities in armaments production established by Hitler for the *Wehrmacht* between September and November 1939. It was instead the Junkers 88 programme of the *Luftwaffe* and the massive expansion of ammunition production for the *Heer* that received the 'special level' classification which denoted absolute manufacturing priority in the allocation of resources. All equipment pertaining to the *Schnellen Truppen* (Fast Troops, the tanks and motorised infantry) received the lower classification of Priority Level 1A. The preference given to ammunition production amounted to some 70 per cent of resource allocation awarded to the *Heer*, leaving the remainder to satisfy the demands of all other needs of the Army.

There is no clearer pointer to the lowly strategic aspirations of Hitler and the OKH (Oberkommando des Heeres, the High Command) in the months before the end of 1939. These priorities focused on the need to service an early campaign in the West which sought to do little other than to fulfil the objectives of the initial drafts for *Fall Gelb* as prepared by the OKH. This envisaged an offensive through Holland and Belgium to capture the channel ports and secure landing fields for the *Luftwaffe* to begin a bombing campaign against the United Kingdom. It is also indicative of the reality that the *Panzerwaffe* was, even after its performance in Poland, still not perceived by Hitler or the majority of conservatively-minded officers in the higher echelons of the *Heer* as the potentially war-winning weapon it came to be viewed as after June 1940.

Even though production of the all-important medium Panzers increased between October 1939 and May 1940 (see table below), the actual numbers produced on a monthly basis were still lamentable. German industry was unable, at this stage of the conflict, to increase the output of tanks much beyond the low levels illustrated. This was even after the implementation of a tank production drive begun in the autumn of 1939. With the decision in February 1940 to phase out from the combat units all *Panzer* IIIs of the early *Ausfürung* (*Ausf* in short, meaning model or mark) A-D development models (with only the specialised Pz III Ausf D Pz.Bef.Wg seeing further service in the French campaign), the 381 *Panzer* IIIs fielded by the *Panzerwaffe* at the start of *Fall Gelb* were all therefore of the later Ausf E, F and G.

German tank production October 1939 – May 1940
Production of the Panzer 1b had ceased in June 1937

Month	Panzer II	Panzer III	Panzer IV
October 1939	8	40	20
November	2	35	11
December	0	42	14
January 1940	0	42	20
February	unknown	unknown	unknown
March	unknown	unknown	unknown
April	12 (9 flammenwerfer)	51	11
May	12 (12 flammenwerfer)	65	11
Totals	55	275	87

These mounted increased armour protection and were equipped with a superior torsion bar suspension system. Further incremental improvements were introduced in each succeeding model. Although a 50mm KwK L/42 tank gun had been developed prior to the war, and had been available to be mounted on the Model F which went into production in September 1939, the Army chose to retain the 37mm KwK L/46 cannon for the purposes of ammunition compatibility with the anti-tank units. Only the last 100 of the 435 Ausf Fs produced were equipped with the more powerful weapon. The first 50 of the Pz III Ausf G, which went into production alongside the Ausf F in April 1940, also mounted the smaller calibre gun (although after the fall of France many of the surviving Ausf E, F and early G were refitted with the 50mm gun). All *Panzer* IIIs in service on 10 May 1940 therefore mounted only the 37mm weapon.

As the understudy to the *Panzer* III, and primarily designated as a 'support tank for it on combat operations', the *Panzer* IV was never intended to be produced in as great a number. Although there were more Pz IVs than Pz IIIs in service on 1 September 1939, the 290 in service for the western campaign were just 79 more than were used in *Fall Weiss*. This was reflective of this machine being allocated a lower production priority than the lighter Pz III, which was earmarked as the primary equipment of the Panzer Divisions. Indeed, with a maximum of just 20 a month leaving the Krupp-Gruson works, the Pz IV was virtually hand-built, the production methods employed being quite archaic. Every Pz III and IV constructed required the expenditure of some 4,000 man-hours, this extremely high figure being halved only with the introduction of more rational production methods later in the war. Nonetheless, there were sufficient Pz IVs of the Ausf A through D variants in service by May 1940 to permit every tank unit to field a medium tank company of between six and eleven machines in what was, by the beginning of the western campaign, an expanded *Panzerwaffe*.

a) Reorganisation:

By May 1940 there were ten Panzer Divisions in service, four more than at the start of the Polish campaign. This was not the result of a headlong rush to expand the *Panzerwaffe* following its success in Poland but rather the planned implementation of a memorandum issued by the head of the *Heer* in November 1938. At that time the stated intention was to raise a force of nine Panzer Divisions, the other four being created by conversion of the extant four *leichte* (light) divisions into fully fledged tank divisions in the autumn of 1939. The dates of conversion and the new designations of these formations were as follows:

PANZERWAFFE

On 12 Sept. 1939:	1 Light Division	became	6. Panzer Division.*
On 18 Oct. 1939:	2 Light Division	became	7. Panzer Division.+
On 16 Oct. 1939:	3 Light Division	became	8. Panzer Division.+
On 3 Jan. 1940:	4 Light Division	became	9. Panzer Division.

* This division was the only one equipped with the Pz.kpfw.35(t) in May 1940
+ These two divisions were equipped with the Pz.kpfw.38(t) in May 1940

Falling outside the planned expansion programme, which in 1938 had 'fixed' the maximum size of the *Panzerwaffe* at these nine divisions, was 10. *Panzer Division*. This was raised ostensibly as an 'occupation force' following the occupation of the rump of Czechoslovakia in the early spring of 1939. However, the need for extra tanks had seen this formation fielded as a distinct Panzer Division during the Polish campaign, and it continued to serve as such thereafter until its destruction in Tunisia in May 1943.

The hiatus between the end of the Polish campaign and the onset of the western one had seen the introduction of a number of new types that would play a significant role in the development of the German tank arm through to the end of the war.

b) New equipment
Hanomag Sdkfz.251 *Schutzenpanzerwagen*

It had always been an integral part of Guderian's notion of the Armoured Formation that it would be a self-contained all-arms unit. Not just composed of Panzers, it would be supported by its own organic motorised infantry and supporting artillery. In that, the expectation was that such equipment would operate in conjunction with the Panzers so something more than a wheeled vehicle would be needed to give the proper mobility, cross country performance and protection to accompanying infantry.

While theory could propose, only German industry could dispose and, in the case of the former the planned acquisition of a fully-tracked armoured troop carrier was simply beyond its capacity and regarded as far too expensive. In 1937 a compromise, in the form of an armoured body fitted to the chassis of the pre-existing SdKfz 11 3 ton medium half-track artillery tractor led to the emergence of a vehicle that was to become as synonymous with the operations of the *Panzerwaffe* as the tanks themselves. Initially designated the *Gepanzerte Mannschafts Transportwagen* or armoured personnel carrier, and later by its more common title of *Schutzenpanzerwagen* (SPW for short, and meaning armour protected transport vehicle), the first prototype of this important vehicle emerged in 1938. Ordered into production and built by the firm of Hanomag, the very first Sd.Kfz 251s entered service with a single company of the infantry regiment of 1. *Panzer Division* in the spring of 1939. 232 of the Ausf A were produced in 1939 and a further 337 of the Ausf B in 1940. Although few saw service in Poland, the limited experience derived from their combat employment was translated into a new training manual for the type during the winter of 1939/40. By May 1940, enough SPWs were available to see service with other Panzer Divisions and the 251 was already spawning the first of a huge number of variants – no fewer than twenty-two – which would see service on all the *Heer*'s battlefields up to 1945. It would only be at the start of the Russian campaign that enough of these machines would be available to contribute in a significant fashion to the effectiveness of the performance of the Panzer Divisions.

It should then come as no surprise that this vehicle was to prove outstandingly successful, and even though production expanded substantially in the years after 1940, the demand for the SPW always exceeded the ability of German industry to satisfy. The three other new machines fielded by the *Heer* for *Fall Gelb* were the progenitors of types that would play an increasingly important and organic role within the tank divisions as the war continued. Of these, the most important was the *Sturmgeschutz* III.

Sturmgeschutz III

The invasion of France and the Low Countries witnessed the commitment to combat of a fighting vehicle that was, during the course of the next five years, to acquire a formidable reputation as a tank killer. It had not, however, been planned to fulfil this role. The *Sturmgeschutz* III (abbreviated to StuG III) or assault gun, as it became better known, was designed as a tracked, armoured, artillery support vehicle for infantry formations on the battlefield. The order for this machine was issued by the *Heeres Waffenamt* (army ordnance dept), on 15 June 1936, the specification calling for a vehicle mounting a gun of at least 75mm with a limited traverse. The selected weapon was modified by Krupp from the short-barrelled 75mm L/24 *Kampfwagenkanone* (although designated in the StuG III as *Sturmkanone*) produced for the *Panzer* IV, thus enabling the new assault gun to carry armour piercing as well as high explosive shells. Although the requirement called for all round armour protection, the top of the superstructure was left open. The chassis chosen for this new machine was that of the *Panzer* III. The requirement that it be no higher off the ground than the height of an average man reflected the absence of any turret and imparted to the StuG the low silhouette which was to help make it such a successful design.

The first StuG test battery was established in 1937. By then, the new machine had acquired an armoured roof. It had also been determined that this new weapon would be fielded by the artillery and not the *Panzerwaffe*, with units employing this type being designated as *Sturmartillerie* (assault artillery). However, all training on assault guns was halted in the autumn of 1938 and the project went into limbo until combat experience in Poland led to an urgent call for the StuG to be fielded forthwith. Daimler Benz delivered the first 6 machines in February 1940 and a further 24 by the end of May, when manufacture of the Ausf A ceased with a switch to the production of the improved Ausf B, which came on line in June. No Ausf Bs were available for service in the western campaign. They were organised into six-vehicle batteries, only four of which actually saw service in *Fall Gelb*. These were designated *Sturmbatteries* 640, 659, 660 and 665 with the latter being allocated to the elite *Infanterie-Regiment Grossdeutschland*, where it was redesignated 16. *Sturmbatterie* and became an integral part of the formation thereafter. The successful debut of the assault gun saw both a reorganisation of batteries into self-contained battalions and an expansion in the number of formations fielding the type after the French campaign.

Other types

The introduction of the 150mm *sIG33(Sf) auf Panzerkampfwagen 1* Ausf *B* marked the first attempt by the Germans to field a self-propelled gun for the specific purpose of providing direct artillery support for armoured infantry serving alongside the Panzers. As such, it was the progenitor of the later and much more successful *Wespe* and *Hummel* models, which appeared in 1943.

The firm of Alkett was tasked with the conversion of a number of obsolescent *Panzer* 1 Ausf B tanks into self-propelled guns in early 1940. The 150mm weapon designated for this new type was the largest calibre ever classified as an infantry gun. To accommodate this heavy weapon, the turret and superstructure of the *Panzer* 1 was removed and replaced by a high, thinly armoured, box shaped armoured shield within which the sIG33 weapon was emplaced, wheels and all. The box shield was open above and to the rear, providing little protection for the crew of four. The finished product looked cumbersome, and the weight of the heavy gun overstressed the light chassis of the *Panzer* 1. Nonetheless, the thirty-eight produced in February 1940 were allocated to six newly-raised Heavy Infantry Gun Companies, with one of each being attached to each of six Panzer Divisions for the offensive against France and the Low Countries. One of the more notable scenes from the *Deutsche Wochenschau* newsreels covering events in May and June 1940 shows a single one of these SP guns advancing along a French street supported by infantry. It then stops and fires, demolishing the house directly in front of it. The spectacle is quite impressive, as no doubt the *Propaganda Kompanie* cameraman intended it to be!

Also making its debut in May 1940 was the first in a long line of what would prove to be a vitally important class of machine to see service with the *Heer* throughout World War II. The concept of the *PanzerJäger* was to provide mobility to an anti-tank gun by emplacing it within a thinly-armoured splinter shield on a tracked chassis, with the primary task of such a machine being to protect infantry from enemy armour. *PanzerJäger* were an integral part of the *Panzerwaffe* and their crews wore the same black uniform with its pink piping denoting the arm of service.

The first in this class of vehicle to see service was yet another conversion of the PzKpfw 1 Ausf B, with later types of this class employing the chassis of the PzKpfw II and the PzKpfw 38(t). The weapon selected for this first 'tank hunter' was the Czech 47mm cannon P.U.V. 36 anti-tank gun, which was appropriated by the Germans in large numbers in 1939 and classified by them as the 4.7cm Pak 36(t). The weapon had a marginally higher muzzle velocity and fired a heavier shell, being

Continued on page 22

THE STATE OF THE PANZERWAFFE

*This Pz II Ausf B or C photographed in Arras in May 1940 has been uparmoured by fitting a squared-off appliqué bow over its original rounded bow and a shaped plate on to its turret front.
It is so dusty that no trace can be seen of the two-tone grey and brown camouflage. Cloth has been wrapped around its guns to keep the dust out of them. Its tactical number II02 is painted in white.*

PANZERWAFFE

French destruction of river bridges made little difference to the German advance, because German troops were highly trained in building replacements. Here a Pz IV Ausf C crosses an expertly-built pontoon bridge.

The 8.8cm Flak 18 Sfl mounted on a 12 tonne Zugkraftwagen (unfortunately with no official abbreviation) was designed as a 'bunkerknacker' to knock out enemy bunkers but also proved very effective as a tank destroyer. All of the few built were used by the 1st Kompanie of PanzerJägerAbteilung 8 (abbreviated to PzJagAbt 8 and meaning Tank Hunter Batallion 8) and this example was knocked out near Sedan during the French campaign; some accounts say that it was the victim of a bombing error by a Stuka. Traces of its grey and brown camouflage can be seen but the only visible markings are its white outline cross and the number plates on its front. Its '88' is a specially-modified version of the anti-aircraft gun.

Ein abgebrannter deutscher Panzerjäger bei Sedan

PANZERWAFFE

THE STATE OF THE PANZERWAFFE

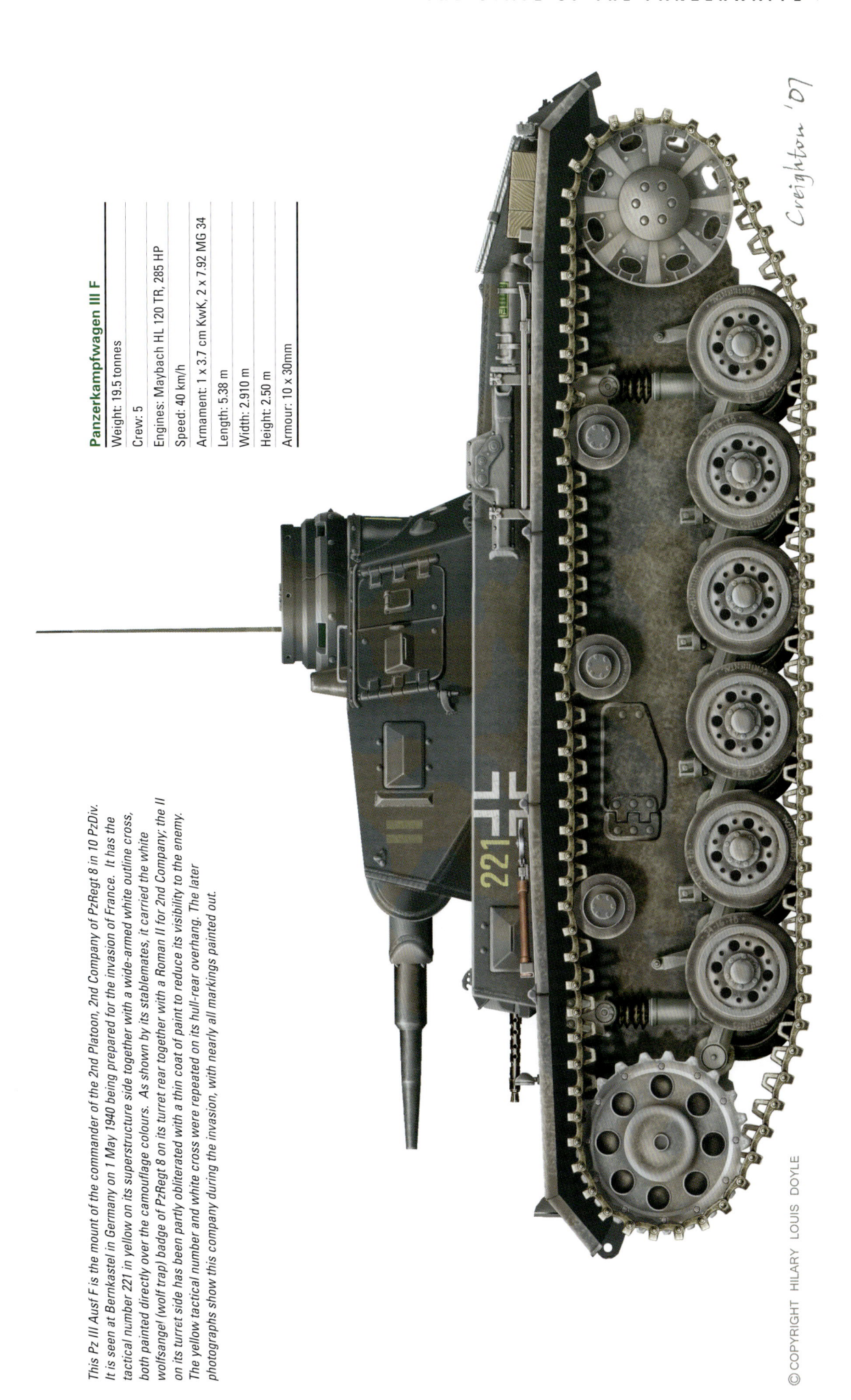

Panzerkampfwagen III F
Weight: 19.5 tonnes
Crew: 5
Engines: Maybach HL 120 TR, 285 HP
Speed: 40 km/h
Armament: 1 x 3.7 cm KwK, 2 x 7.92 MG 34
Length: 5.38 m
Width: 2.910 m
Height: 2.50 m
Armour: 10 x 30mm

This Pz III Ausf F is the mount of the commander of the 2nd Platoon, 2nd Company of PzRegt 8 in 10 PzDiv. It is seen at Bernkastel in Germany on 1 May 1940 being prepared for the invasion of France. It has the tactical number 221 in yellow on its superstructure side together with a wide-armed white outline cross, both painted directly over the camouflage colours. As shown by its stablemates, it carried the white wolfsangel (wolf trap) badge of PzRegt 8 on its turret rear together with a Roman II for 2nd Company; the II on its turret side has been partly obliterated with a thin coat of paint to reduce its visibility to the enemy. The yellow tactical number and white cross were repeated on its hull-rear overhang. The later photographs show this company during the invasion, with nearly all markings painted out.

therefore superior in range and penetrative power, to the 37mm Pak 36 anti-tank gun which was the standard anti-tank gun of the *Heer* and the weapon employed in a modified form in the early *Panzer* III. Although 132 were produced by the firm of Daimler-Benz from March 1940 through to February 1941, only a small number saw service in the French campaign in a number of *Heeres PanzerJägerAbteilung*. The majority of this type saw service after the fall of France. They were later employed in Russia and the Western Desert.

The rival armour: Char versus Panzer
Given the rapidity of the German victory over France, Belgium and Holland and the pivotal role played by the Panzer Divisions in bringing this about, the superficial judgement at the time was that German tanks must not only have been more numerous than those of the Allied armies, but also superior to them. However, we will need to qualify how this term was understood. For the purposes of immediate explanation, we will assume that 'superior' was employed as a shorthand for greater numbers, heavier armour and more effective firepower.

a) Numbers
There is no question that, as regards the first of these greater numbers, the Western Allies possessed at the beginning of *Fall Gelb* a decided superiority in the numbers of tanks that they could field compared to the Germans at the beginning of *Fall Gelb*. While full breakdowns by tank type and their totals for each of the ten Panzer Divisions are provided in tabular form, the overall number of tanks deployed by the *Panzerwaffe* for combat operations on 10 May 1940 amounted to 2,582 machines of all types. This was exceeded by a considerable margin by the number possessed by the French Army alone. The French maintained a tank park of some 4,360 machines of all types, of which 250 were stationed overseas in their colonial territories at that date. By far and away the bulk and best of France's armoured strength was stationed on the north-east Front ready to deploy into Belgium once news had been received of the opening of the German offensive. Not only did the French possess a quantitative advantage over the *Panzerwaffe* in theatre, but also many of their tanks were also superior in the thickness of armour protection they carried and in the calibre of the armament they mounted. Even the Germans themselves accepted that a number of the tank types being fielded by the French Army were superior to their own, the best example of this being the Somua S-35 cavalry medium tank, regarded by many armour pundits of the time as one of the finest in the world.

Although of lesser importance, the armoured contributions of the British and the Belgians served to raise total Allied numbers to just over 4,000 machines. This numerical strength explains why General Gamelin was so confident that the Allied tank force would crush that of the Germans when they invaded Belgium *en masse* which, as we have seen, he was absolutely convinced they would.

b) Armour
The greatest disparity between the tanks of the Germans and the French lay in the area of armour protection. Even the 'heaviest' Panzer in service at the time of the invasion of France – the *Panzer* IV Ausf D – weighing in at a modest 18 tons, mounted armour no thicker than 30mm across its frontal arc, although the gun mantlet was formed of 35mm of rolled armour plate. The equivalent machine in the French Army at the time – the Char B1 Bis – at nearly double the weight of a Pz, had frontal armour double the thickness of the Pz at 60mm. At the time of the German offensive in the west, the two tanks planned to become the standard equipment of the *Panzerwaffe* were woefully protected.

At the other end of the spectrum, the most numerous German tank was the diminutive *Panzer* I light tank, whose maximum armour thickness of just 13mm was not even enough to withstand a high velocity rifle bullet. It was to prove appallingly vulnerable to every calibre of gun mounted on French tanks and to Allied anti-tank guns. This machine, and the later *Panzer* II light tank – the second most numerous German tank to see service in the French campaign – had also proved vulnerable in Poland to enemy anti-tank rifle fire by virtue of their very thin armour. Remedial action was undertaken in the months following the Polish campaign to improve the protection of the *Panzer* II by the addition of rivetted plates of 20mm armour. Although only some 70 per cent of the *Panzer* II inventory had been improved in this fashion by 10 May, this did serve to increase the maximum thickness across the vital frontal arc of those machines to approximately 35mm, and this enabled the Germans to rectify the design's most evident weakness. Nonetheless, both machines were castigated by their operators in the French campaign as being 'unfit for combat'.

Although the French Army was still deploying quite a number of its early AMC and AMR light tanks whose armour was equivalent to that of the *Panzer* I and II, the most numerous and modern machines of this class, namely the Renault 35, Hotchkiss 35/39 and Renault 35, all mounted a maximum of 40mm of armour as standard. Thus, the most common French light tank in May 1940 carried thicker armour than did the heaviest Panzer!

It was, however, when the Germans faced the British Matilda II that they encountered the tank bearing the heaviest armour of any in the 1940 campaign. Although the thinnest carried by this machine was just 20mm, found on its hull and turret tops, the 78mm of its cast hull front and nose rendered it invulnerable to any weapon carried by any German AFV, in 1940. As was to be found later when it was also encountered in the Western Desert, the 88mm Flak 18/36 gun was needed to despatch the beast!

While in the aftermath of defeat the myth that the Germans were fielding more numerous and better armoured tanks became a convenient excuse to explain away the rapid Allied collapse, the matter was actually made worse by virtue of the fact that the weapons carried by these same Allied tanks were also better than those of the Panzers!

c) Firepower
The twin 7.92mm MG-13 machine guns carried by the *Panzer* I rendered the type suitable for little more than infantry support, whilst the 20mm KwK L/30 cannon of the *Panzer* II was ineffective in penetrating all of the French types. However, it could do so with the armour of the British light and cruiser tanks, and these were penetrated at all ranges. In post-campaign analysis, the 37mm calibre gun mounted on the *Panzer* Mark III and the Pak36 anti-tank gun were castigated as being inadequate to penetrate enemy tanks. It was for this reason that this weapon acquired the unflattering sobriquet of the army's 'door knocker'. Numerous reports spoke of 37mm shells from both weapons simply bouncing off the armour of tanks like the Somua and Char B1-Bis. What emerged as the most effective tank mounted weapon against enemy tanks in the French campaign was the low velocity, 75mm KwK37 L/24 gun carried on the *Panzer* IV. This weapon had not been designed for this purpose, as it was essentially a low velocity howitzer appropriate for the Panzer's designated task of supporting infantry and other tanks. As the largest calibre weapon carried by any of the Panzers, it fired the heaviest shell and, when employing the limited number of *Sprenggranate* (armour piercing shells) ammunition it carried in combat (with the majority carried being HE), it was able to take on and defeat the Somua S-35, albeit only up to a range of 600 metres. Beyond this distance, the effectiveness of the weapon fell off rapidly. However, even the 75mm weapon found difficulty penetrating the heavier frontal armour of the Char B1. One German officer later observed that in a one to one with either of these French tanks, even the *Panzer* IV would have little chance of success.

On paper, which is in terms of a straight comparison in the size and effectiveness of weaponry, most French tanks also had an advantage across the board relative to those carried by the Panzers. Apart from the older AMR 35 which mounted, like the *Panzer* I, nothing other than a machine gun, all other French designs fielded weapons of 25mm calibre or more. As the most numerous type in service with the French Army in 1940, the H-35 class of light cavalry tanks carried a 37mm or 40mm weapon, double the size of that carried by their German counterparts. Even the obsolescent FT-17, dating to the First World War and still in service in some numbers in 1940, albeit mainly in reserve units, mounted a 37mm gun. The two most formidable French machines – namely the Somua S-35 and Char B1-Bis – both mounted a variant of the excellent French 47mm anti-tank gun in their turrets, while the latter also disposed of a 75mm weapon in its lower front hull.

The 2 pounder QF (quick firing) gun was the main armament of the British Army cruiser tanks and of the Matilda II heavy infantry support tank encountered by the Germans in the French Campaign. Although later castigated by its users in the Western Desert, primarily for its lack of a high explosive shell, the 2 pdr was none the less regarded as one of the best weapons of its type in the world in 1940. A barrel length of 50 calibres allowed the gun to fire an AP round at quite a high velocity, thus permitting British tankers to hit the more lightly armoured German Panzers at a greater range. It was superior to its nearest enemy equivalent, the 37mm weapon mounted on the *Panzer* III.

Char versus Panzer: The factors that really mattered!
Notwithstanding the 'on paper' superiority of French armour in particular areas, the 1940 campaign would illustrate the degree to which these were degraded by a whole series of other factors. These ranged from French Army doctrine and organisation through to general design limitations and other issues, all of which combined to render the whole, in the crucible of war, to be substantially less than the sum of its parts.

It is a truism that French armour doctrine at the start of the Second World War was in essence no different to that at the end of the First. The roles of the tank were that of infantry support and the provision of a mechanised equivalent of the cavalry. These two suppositions governed all aspects of tank unit organisation, their use, design and development in the inter-war period. It meant that when faced with a technologically inferior enemy whose tank arm was predicated upon a far more dynamic concept of the use of armour and air power, the French were unable to respond in an effective way and went down to defeat.

Cited as a maxim in pre-war French Service Regulations, tanks had to observe the requirement of only moving as fast as the infantry they were supporting. In consequence, the specifications issued for new machines to fulfil the support role rarely required that they have a maximum speed beyond 17 mph. These machines formed the core of the five Light Cavalry Divisions in 1940. These comprised a light mechanised brigade equipped with the H-35/R-35/H-38/H-39 tanks, Panhard armoured cars and mechanised infantry. It is a measure of their anachronistic structure that they still included a brigade of cavalry.

The Cavalry Division analogue was to be found in the three *Divisions Légères Mécaniques* (abbreviated hereafter to DLM). These light mechanised divisions were seen conceptually as mechanised cavalry. Their primary role was to advance to the fore of the main force and screen its movements – a role that Joachim Murat, Napoleon's commander of cavalry, would have related to without difficulty save for the fact that these steeds were of steel and not flesh and blood! Fielding a mixture of Hotchkiss light tanks and the more formidable Somua S-35s, two of these divisions would be involved in the largest tank clash of the campaign at Hannut in Belgium on 12 and 13 May.

Evidence, however, that the contribution played by the *Panzerwaffe* in the rapid defeat of Poland had not gone by way of the board in France can be seen in how between September 1939 and May 1940 the French had moved very quickly to create their own equivalent of the Panzer Division. Four *Divisions Cuirassées Rapide* (hereafter abbreviated to DCR) were set up in short order. Three were already part of the order of battle on 10 May. The fourth, as yet still forming, was under the command of a certain Colonel Charles de Gaulle (one of the few minds in the French camp in the 1930s who had been in tune with German armoured developments and had argued for the same in France). With a mechanised infantry battalion and two battalions of artillery, the core of these formations was built around two battalions of 60 Char B1 Bis. This was the premier tank of the French Army in 1940. However, it had not been designed for *rapide*. Its original specification had called for a machine to provide infantry support! The top speed of just 18mph illustrates the point. More numerous were 78 Hotchkiss H-39s that were also organised in two battalions. When enabled to take up static positions, the heavy frontal armour and weapons of French machines enabled them to deal without difficulty with all German tanks – their armour being so weak.

When denied that facility, they succumbed rapidly to the superior movement of the Panzer formation operating in concert with other arms and the *Luftwaffe*. This was bound to happen at any time the Germans effected a breakthrough of the French line – be it held by infantry or armour – because of the latter's attention to the maintenance of contiguous lines. This hangover from the Great War, when trench lines dictated the requirement to preserve a coherent front, contained within it the seeds of many errors made in 1940 by the French Army. By default it conferred many tactical and strategic gains on the Germans, who rapidly and ruthlessly exploited every opportunity provided when this effect of this anachronistic doctrine was employed.

Although the new DCRs appeared formidable on paper, they had been set up to emulate a formation whose armour doctrine was alien to the French military mind. It would take more than a few months and a reorganisation of assets to copy what the Germans had done in Poland. Herein is to be seen a profound weakness in the design of French armour that was to impact on its ability to duplicate the mobility of the Panzer Divisions in Poland. We have already alluded to the slowness of French tank designs. It was also the case that the efficiency of any Char in battle in 1940 was seriously handicapped by the one-man turret they all carried. To the commander of the vehicle, who had to identify the target, also fell the tasks of aiming the gun, rotating the turret, loading the gun and firing it. Nor was he helped by the poor view provided for him by limited optics. However, all of the aforementioned were then compounded by the slow traverse of the turret.

Contrast this with German design practice. Unlike their French counterparts, the German medium Panzers had crews of five men. Representing, as they did, the machines that would see the *Panzerwaffe* through to 1943, and in the case of the Pz IV through to the defeat in 1945, the insistence by the *Heeres Waffenamt* on a three-man turret design was proved by experience. A commander, loader and aimer were deemed to provide the best arrangement for the division of labour in carrying out those tasks, thereby providing the optimum efficiency of the workload of a crew when in battle. With the commander able to observe events from his cupola and communicate his orders via a throat microphone, this permitted the Panzer to rapidly move and shift both vehicle and main armament from target to target. The trump card, however, for the German way of war in 1940 was the radios carried by all Panzers, but very few Chars. In a real sense, they were the war winner.

It was the onboard radios carried by all Panzers that permitted them to manoeuvre rapidly on the battlefield to take account of contingencies as they arose. It was accepted even in 1940 that 'the primary method of command in combat' was the radio. Drilling in the use of this medium was deemed by the *Panzerwaffe* to be as important as firing accurately. By 1940, the *Panzerwaffe* had had years of practice in war games and operations in which to develop their radio procedures and inculcate the protocols of such in their tank crews. A short insight into the sophistication of such methods and their common usage through the tank arm in 1940 can be gleaned from this instruction manual extract:

'Movements are carried out according to radio command, previous orders or signals (although radio was accepted as being the most workable means of command – author comment). On the order to move out, all tanks start moving uniformly and at first, straight ahead. If a change of formation is desired at the same time as the start of the move, the formation order is given first, followed by the order to move out. Distances, intervals and formation are assumed while driving …. When changing direction of the march, the commander orders 'Follow me!' or 'Direction of march is…!' while giving point or compass bearing. If a formation change is to take place at the same time, the march direction is given first, followed by the new formation. Platoons that have four, instead of five, tanks execute these formations and manoeuvres in analogous fashion'.

The degree of control implicit in such a short extract and the sophistication required to effect it betokens a great expertise in radio employment. Herein lies the French bafflement at the ability of the Germans to move their tanks around *en masse* and effect a rapid concentration of effort and firepower where they desired it. This is hardly surprising when very few French tanks actually possessed radios. Apart from a cultural obsession with radio security, which provides one explanation as to why they were not fitted in their tanks, the other problem arose again directly out of the perception that tanks were only to provide support for the infantry. In such circumstances, radios were not necessary, signal flags would suffice and, once drawn up in their static lines facing the enemy, it was thought to be enough for an officer or runner to move from tank to tank passing on orders in person by word of mouth!

The sophisticated German radio net went beyond tank to tank. It also permitted a degree of communication between ground and air that had never been seen before. Attached to the Panzer Divisions were *Fliegerleittrupps* – tactical air control parties – which were provided with wheeled vehicles. At this juncture of the war there were too few SPWs available to be fitted out for this role, although they would become a more familiar sight from 1941 onward. Their task was to be in close proximity to the advancing Panzers. When the tank divisions' own towed artillery could not eliminate a target, the *Fliegerleit offizier* – the air control officer – elicited what air support was available and contacted the pilots on their frequency. In 1940, it was the Stuka and the Henschel Hs-123 which provided this help, with the bulk of the air support being provided by the former. The air control officer would then talk the pilots into the area so that they could recognise the target. In the meantime, troops with the Panzers would have demarcated their own positions relative to that of the enemy by laying out on the ground special identification panels. It was later claimed that the support given to Guderian's thrust to the channel saw the most effective use of air support of the war, with Stukas being on hand to deal with targets within 15-20 minutes of being called.

A Pz II Ausf b of 5 PzDiv in France. The tactical number 802 is still displayed on the rhomboid plates used in Poland, but the division sign of a yellow X on the back of the fighting compartment and the wide-armed white outline cross beside it prove that the photograph was taken during the French campaign. The lower case b of its Ausf designation is a reminder of its pre-production origin, the early Pz II series with experimental suspension using lower case while the larger-wheeled mass-produced Pz IIs used upper case Ausf designations.

A SdKfz 251 Ausf A of 5 PzDiv in France. The yellow X of the division sign and white tactical sign of a motorised infantry unit, with 9 beside it for the Kompanie, and the hollow white cross on its side, would also appear on its rear. The object on which one of the men is resting his elbow is the front swinging arm for fitting a machine gun.

The British equivalent of the Pz I was the Matilda I, also armed with a machine gun – only one against the Pz I's two – but much more heavily armoured for its role of overrunning enemy positions. This is Dennis of 4 Royal Tank Regiment, carrying the British Expeditionary Force's white identification squares as well as its name. The square on the turret rear has two diagonal lines, possibly red and probably identifying a platoon commander's tank.

Germany was also keen to provide its troops with mechanised anti-aircraft cover. Here a unit prepares to leave its barracks in Germany for an exercise in February 1940. These are SdKfz 7/1 half-tracks, the /1 indicating their adaption to carry 3.7 cm anti-aircraft guns – the barrel of one can be seen pointing skywards. These vehicles were able to travel with tanks, or supply convoys, and spring into instant action to protect them from air attack in a way that towed guns could never match. A point of interest is that although the front half-track carries the yellow emblem of 4 PzDiv on its front mudguard beside the white tactical symbol of an anti-aircraft unit, it has a Luftwaffe number plate.

THE STATE OF THE PANZERWAFFE

A Sturmgeschuetze (Stug for short, and meaning 'assault gun') III Ausf A seen in France. These vehicles mounted a short 7.5 cm gun in a new superstructure on the Pz III chassis and were designed as mobile artillery to accompany the infantry in battle. Its crew wear a grey version of the black Panzer uniform.

A PzJag I unit waits for orders on a road in France. The vehicles carry an impressive array of spare wheels, tracks and other items.

A Matilda II infantry tank captured from the BEF. It has the raised suspension fitted to some of these tanks, and also a trench-crossing skid at its rear. Unfortunately its name is not readable so its unit cannot be identified, but its two tone medium and dark green camouflage scheme can be seen.

A British A9 Cruiser Mark I left behind in France after Dunkirk.

(This page and opposite) As well as the self-propelled 'bunkerknacker' Flak 18 8.8 cm guns there were towed versions as well, specially modified to allow them to be fired while still mounted on their wheels. These photographs were taken in Czechoslovakia in October 1938 but were not available for the production of the first volume in this series. At that time the guns were still in the early three-colour camouflage but the tractors, built after them, were in the grey and brown scheme.

THE STATE OF THE PANZERWAFFE 27

A Pz 38(t) Ausf B in Luxembourg. The rhomboid-shaped item with holes in it is not an external fitting but an ammunition bin for its main gun, and must have been removed while some work was carried out inside. The divisions between its grey and brown camouflage colours can be seen on the turret and hull front.

THE STATE OF THE PANZERWAFFE

Although Germany was mechanising its troops as quickly as possible, the process was never completed. Here a mechanised artillery unit, with an SdKfz 11 half-track gun tractor towing a 10.5 cm leFH 18 light field howitzer, passes a horsedrawn unit with the same type of gun. The marking on the half-track appears to be an L, presumably the gun letter.

This Pz III Ausf G was seen on an exercise ground in Germany before the Western campaign. It has no markings except its hollow white cross and so may be very newly issued to its unit.

PANZERWAFFE

The French Char de Rupture 2C was built in the 1920s as a 'breakthrough tank' but kept in service until 1940. They never saw action, thanks to rail transport breakdowns as well as Luftwaffe attacks, and '99' (below right) was overrun by PzRegt 10 which proudly emblazoned its name on both sides. Despite being stationary and without crews some of them were shot up. '98' (above and above right) was one of these and the resulting damage made a popular photographic subject for German troops – 'see what our arms can do to the French monster tank!' seems a likely comment.

An SdKfz 251 Ausf A of 1 PzDiv followed by a column of prisoners in Flanders. This is a rare image of the unarmoured troop carrier version on active service. It is distinguishable by the plain flat plates of the vision ports in its sides, which had noticeable bulges in their armoured form. Its only visible marking is the yellow 41 on its front mudguard, the division sign and any other markings being on the port mudguard which is out of the picture.

Sieg im Westen

FALL GELB began at 5:35 am on 10 May 1940. It was initiated by wide-ranging *Luftwaffe* operations against targets throughout France and the Low Countries. For the Dutch and Belgian governments, the aerial assault banished any pretensions they may have retained that their neutrality would be respected by Germany. At 6:00 am, the Dutch government formally requested that the Allied powers assist them in resisting the German attack. Barely fifty minutes later, following reports of German troop incursions across his border, King Leopold reluctantly invited the French and British to enter Belgium and help defend his nation.

It was as if a switch had been thrown. Once the news had been received at French Army Headquarters in Vincennes of the Dutch and Belgian requests, Gamelin gave the green light to initiate the 'Dyle Plan'. The commander in chief could not have been happier, an emotion shared by the higher echelons of the British and French forces. General Andre Corap, commander of the French Ninth Army (whose command would be savaged within the week by the German drive through the Ardennes) articulated in smug fashion the sentiment of many of his brother officers, when he boasted that 'this is the moment we have been waiting for'. For Gamelin and his colleagues, the presumption that the German offensive drive could only come through Belgium had become an article of faith and, as *they* saw matters unfolding, this is exactly what was happening. All over France, the sentiment was the same.

In bistros around Paris veterans of the Great War celebrated, saying that the Germans would break their teeth against the Maginot Line. A Danish journalist who was in Paris on 10 May recalls that the city was 'bubbling with enthusiasm. On the streets and cafés, in the press and on the radio, there was jubilation over the blunder that Germany had just committed'.

As British and French officers of the First Army Group, under the command of General Billotte, pored over the missive of orders that contained the march-plan for the advance to the Breda-Dyle line, the ponderous Allied war machine began to move. It could not have been otherwise. Governed by a vast proliferation of documentation which had accrued since Plan D had become the agreed Allied design, every minutiae of the advance had been set down, even to the distance that vehicles should maintain from each other as they made progress through Belgium. It was hardly surprising therefore that the last formation in the Allied 'first team' – namely the B.E.F., the British Expeditionary Force – was not ready to begin its own advance until the early afternoon on 11 May. Nor was the speed of their advance helped by the stated requirement that infantry only march at night so as to avoid presenting the *Luftwaffe* with the type of day target they had so savaged in Poland – although this order was quickly rescinded in the face of events.

From the opening day of the offensive, the Allied powers were to display that collective lethargy that would doom them in the face of an enemy imbued with an imperative to speed and rapid movement. The French historian Marcel Bloch put his finger on this cultural failing of the French military establishment when he stated that 'from the beginning to the end of the war, the metronome at headquarters was always set at too slow a beat'. It took less than a day for news to filter through that the enemy was not conforming to Gamelin's master plan, and that the timekeeper at German headquarters was clearly set to operate at a much faster pace.

Although the task of Army Group B had been downgraded in the final variant of Case Yellow, from that of the primary assault formation to a diversionary force, its role was nonetheless absolutely crucial to the successful outcome of the radical German plan now unfolding. As we have seen, Army Group B was tasked with confirming, by the ferocity of its attack, the Allies in their conviction that the *schwerpunkt* of the German offensive in the west was directed towards Holland and Belgium. It was however at a marked disadvantage in terms of the ratio of forces with von Bock fielding just 29 divisions against a combined total, by the time the Allies had fully deployed their own formations alongside those of the Dutch and Belgian armies, of 60 divisions. Nonetheless the huge aerial assault on the Netherlands – which had seen the novel employment of the *Luftwaffe*'s elite *Fallschirmjäger* on the ground and the commitment of 9. *Panzer Division* – all seemed to support this Allied perception. This received further confirmation when enemy armoured formations advanced across the Belgian border with the clear intention of making for the Gembloux Gap, near the industrial town of Namur.

While the number of tanks employed by the three Panzer Divisions deployed by Army Group B amounted to more than a quarter of the total committed by the Germans on 10 May, the prevalence of light Panzers relative to the far smaller numbers of *Panzer*s III and IV illustrated their diversionary role. Their function was to generate enough of a semblance of mass to reinforce the Allies in their conviction that it was only in the Low Countries, and especially Belgium, that the Germans could properly deploy their Panzers. It was to reinforce this perception that for the first three days of the German offensive, the *Luftwaffe* was tasked with giving absolute priority to the support of Army Group B's operations. It was certainly the Allied view, derived from their reading of the manner in which the *Wehrmacht* had conducted its operations in Poland, that where the main enemy effort was, there too the *Luftwaffe* would be operating in support.

Army Group B – von Bock

Division	Panzer I	Panzer II	Panzer III	Panzer IV	Pz. Bef
3. Panzer	117	129	42	26	27
4. Panzer	135	105	40	24	10
9. Panzer	30	54	41	16	12
Totals	282	288	123	66	49

Total of all Panzers in Army Group B 10 May = 808
Total employed by XVI. *Panzerkorps* 10 May = 655
Total number of tankS in 9. PzDiv 10 May = 153

Inasmuch as Gamelin was presuming that the German strategy in Belgium differed little from that ascertained by study of *Aufmarschanweisung* No 2 captured in January, he was confident that the advance of the Panzers would be slowed by the Belgian Army's formidable main defensive line. This was grounded on the deep and straight Albert Canal – which to all intents and purposes functioned as a 38-metre deep anti-tank ditch – which ran north and east from Antwerp to where it joined with the River Meuse, north of Liege. The key position along this line was Eben-Emael, a fortification which was reputed to be the strongest in the world. Its heavily encased artillery was ranged to cover the border town of Maastricht and the three bridges which spanned the canal. The latter had been rigged with explosives and they were to be blown up in the event that they might be captured by the Germans. Given the potential of this position to hold up a German advance predicated on the absolute need for speed, the elimination of Eben-Emael and the rapid capture of the bridges over the canal were clearly the linchpins of their offensive design in Belgium.

Such was the seeming strength of this position that Gamelin had presumed that the Belgians could hold this line for a maximum of five to six days, thus permitting his forces to reach their designated positions along the River Dyle in good time and in good order. His first intimation that matters were not unfolding as he had foreseen came with news that the Belgian Army was pulling back from the Albert Canal, and that German armour was already being reported operating to the west of it little more than twenty-four hours after the start of their offensive. Poor communications – a major contributory factor to the Allied defeat – and the 'fog of war' prevented him from ascertaining what had happened, but the import of this news, if true, was potentially disastrous.

Eban-Emael had been neutralised by the *Luftwaffe* in a remarkable *coup de main* that had used glider-borne troops in the first ever operation of its kind. Not only had this secured the fort in rapid time, but the glider troops had also managed to capture two of the three bridges over the Albert Canal intact. Although a Belgian infantry division had been despatched to recapture the position, by the time it arrived there were already enough Panzers and troops in place to frustrate its attempt.

Although the Belgians had managed to destroy the bridges over the Meuse at Maastricht in the face of the German advance on the opening day of their offensive, the delay caused thereby had been short. Engineer troops had quickly built a replacement, and even before day's end, the backlog of units was being cleared. With the Panzers in the van, Sixth Army began its thrust into Belgium. By 11 May, *Lt. General* Erich Hoeppner's XVI *Panzerkorps*, comprising 3. and 4. *Panzer Divisions* with a combined strength of over 600

SIEG IM WESTEN

Panzerkampfwagen IV D
Weight: 19.5 tonnes
Crew: 5
Engines: Maybach HL 120 TR, 265 HP
Speed: 42 km/h
Armament: 1 x 7.5 cm KwK, 2 x 7.92 MG 34
Length: 5.92 m
Width: 2.83 m
Height: 2.68 m
Armour: 10 x 35mm

This Pz IV Ausf D of 5 PzDiv is seen during a pause in the fighting in France, with its commander still watchful while awaiting the order to advance. It carries the new style of Balkenkreuz as a narrow-armed white outline over its grey and brown camouflage, but still bears its tactical number on the rhomboid plate introduced before the war. The yellow 'X' in front of its cross is the division emblem.

Here a Pz III Ausf E is crossing the Meuse on a pontoon bridge on 14 May 1940. It carries on its turret rear the white 'wolfsangel' (wolf trap) of PzRegt 8 in 10 PzDiv, with a white horizontal bar above it, presumably a company indicator, but since no tactical number is visible this cannot be confirmed.

A Pz III Ausf F of 6 PzDiv crossing a pontoon bridge in Holland, 1940. Its markings are confined to hollow white crosses and the yellow XX of the division emblem on its side. The place and date are interesting, because it is usually thought that the XX did not come into use until 1941.

SIEG IM WESTEN 35

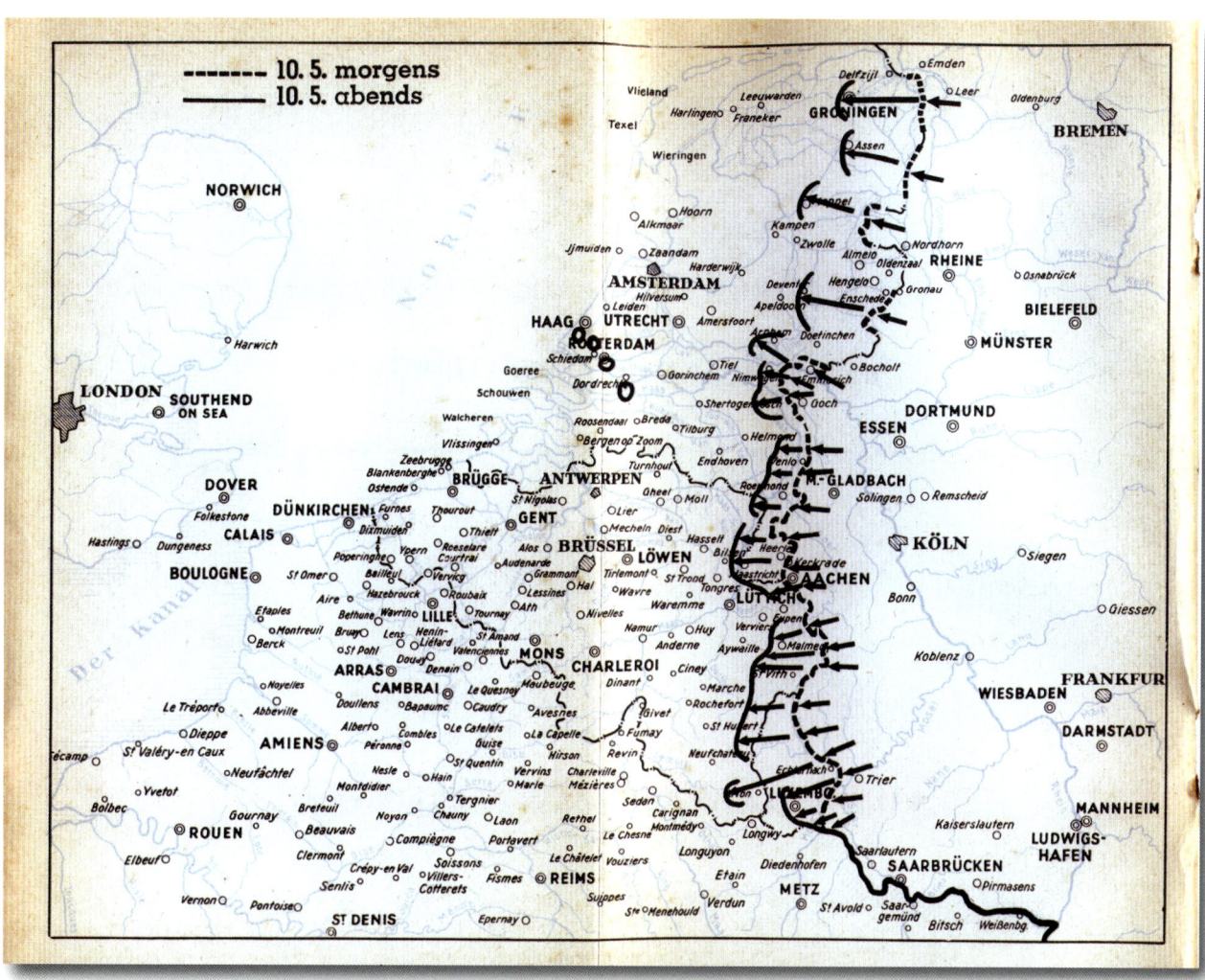

A contemporary map (of a series) published in a German book in 1940 – 'Forward over the Battlefield' on the invasion of France. The map shows the German front line in the morning and the evening of 10 May, the beginning of Fall Gelb. See Publisher's Note at the bottom of page two.

This Dutch observation bunker on the border with Germany was overrun with little damage.

This SdKfz 231 6-wheeled armoured car was photographed in Utrecht, Holland, in May 1940. It still carries on both front mudguards one of the pre-war variations of the tactical sign for a Panzer unit, and its identification letter B is carried on top of its engine deck as well as on the side.

Panzers, had reached the two surviving bridges over the Albert Canal. Because for a time only one was allocated to the *Panzerkorps*, it was 4. *Panzer Division* which crossed first and it was this formation that thrust forward towards the crucial Gembloux Gap.

This fifty-three kilometre-wide region was so called because it was devoid of any natural defences and could thus allow the Germans, should they penetrate it, an optimum entry into central Belgium, which would result in their unhinging the complete Allied defence line along the Dyle. It was for this reason that General Blanchard, as commander of the First Army, had stationed no less than six of his best divisions for the defence of the Gap. It was also intended that a purpose-designed tank obstacle would supplement the defence of the Gap. But very few of these Cointet obstacles, had either been assembled or deployed – those few that had were to be found near the town of Perwez. In consequence, General Blanchard ordered forward Prioux's Cavalry Corps comprising 2nd and 3rd *Divisions Légères Mècaniques* (DLM for short) to provide a screen between the forces assembling to defend the Gap and the oncoming German armour. Prioux was instructed by Blanchard to delay the Germans until at least 15 May, to enable the arriving French infantry divisions to deploy astride the Gap. The encounter between the Prioux Cavalry Corps and Hoeppner's XVI. *Panzerkorps* on 12 and 13 May would make for the first and largest tank battle of the entire western campaign.

By the time of the opening round of this clash on 12 May, Prioux had anchored and dispersed his forces along a thirty-five kilometre line running from the town of Tienen in the north southward through to Huy on the Meuse, to the east of Namur. Each of his two DLMs were deploying three regiments of armour – two each of Hotchkiss H-35 light tanks and one each with the 'formidable' Somua S-35 mediums. The reconnaissance regiment of each division was equipped with the Panhard P-178 armoured car mounting the excellent 25mm cannon, which could penetrate the armour of all the German Panzers. Each DLM also had a regiment of its own organic motorised field artillery supplemented by a further regiment of dragoons mounted on motorcycles and sidecars. In terms of tanks alone, Hoeppner's Panzers would find themselves contending with a French force of some 239 Hotchkiss light tanks and 176 Somua S-35s all of which, on paper, were superior to the German machines.

Although inevitable breakdowns and losses over the previous two days had already reduced to 623 the number of German tanks in XVI. *Panzerkorps*, this nonetheless conferred a superficial numerical superiority over the 415 Hotchkiss and Somuas. In actuality, the Panzers were operating at a distinct disadvantage by reason (as we have seen) of their inferior armament and armour protection. Even if all the light Panzers were still on strength as of 12 May, that would mean that 486 of the total German number were *Panzer*s I and II, whose combat value, as had already been revealed in the Polish campaign, was dubious in the extreme. Nonetheless, 4. *Panzer Division* made contact with the enemy on 12 May, with both divisions being committed to the fight on the following day.

However, the only Panzers with armament able to take on the Somua with any hope of success were the medium *Panzer* IIIs and IVs, of which only 82 of the former and 50 of the latter were available. Nonetheless, this battle was important in demonstrating that factors other than armour and firepower were important in tank clashes of this period. What combat experience demonstrated was that while German tank design was deficient in some areas, it was more advanced in others. Above all, it served to illustrate the manner in which the doctrines of theory and organisation, which had driven the development of the *Panzerwaffe* up to this point, whilst still in a state of flux and being honed in the light of combat experience, were nonetheless proceeding along the correct path. The clash is therefore worthy of some examination in that it prefigured in a similar fashion the problems the Germans would face when encountering superior gun/armour combinations in the summer of 1941, when in the opening stages of Barbarossa, inferior Panzers faced the T-34 and KV series of Soviet tanks. The Germans would overcome them in the same manner as they did the superior French machines encountered in 1940.

ARMOURED CLASH: THE TANK BATTLE AT HANNUT
In keeping with the French Army's doctrinal obsession for adhering to the maintenance of adjoining lines of defence, Prioux's deployment of his two DLM's along the full length of the 35 kilometre front on which he had chosen to make his stand had resulted in his armoured formations being disposed of in a manner likened by one author to 'a string of pearls'. In placing all of his assets in one long line, he thereby had none with which to create a reserve that could be sent to deal with any German breakthrough along that line. Should that occur, then his whole position was in danger of being turned. It therefore fell, in the first instance, to employing the superiority of the gun power and armour protection of his tanks to deny the Germans the immediate breakthrough they sought. And, in that, he succeeded.

Early on 12 May, the vanguard of 4. *Panzer Division* struck at the centre of Prioux's line, at the village of Hannut. This position was held by the tanks and supporting elements of 3rd DLM. Deployed around Hannut and the hamlet of Crehen were approximately 90 Somuas and 140 Hotchkiss tanks, and it was these machines which bore the brunt and weathered the German assault on the first day of this two-day battle. One author has described the opening exchanges:

'At first it was an affair of light forces. Vedettes from the DLMs, spread thinly, encountered the strong Panzer Division's screen. Skirmishes took place between armoured cars, motor cyclists and a few French 25mm anti-tank guns, the latter reporting by radio, 'shooting and scooting' as formidable German combat teams put in an appearance. Delay was inflicted on the Germans at each ambush or as they came to identify and then deploy against successive temporary stop lines'.

The fighting grew in crescendo as the main body of 4. *Panzer*'s armour arrived on scene and entered the fray. However, some three-quarters of the divisional strength consisted of *Panzer* Is and IIs. The inherent vulnerability of these machines was increased by their need to advance over essentially open ground in the face of superior French machines which had taken advantage of the cover given by buildings in the villages and the local terrain. This included hedges within which the tanks could hide and take up ambush positions. This obviated the need for the French tanks to manoeuvre, allowing them to dictate the nature of the battle – forcing the Germans to fight a tank duel in which the French were able to maximise the advantage conferred by their frontal armour and firepower.

The effect on the German light tanks on 12/13 May was catastrophic. Virtually every French weapon from 25mm upward penetrated the 7-13mm of the *Panzer* I. Although the *Panzer* IIs fared somewhat better, especially those that had been uparmoured since the Polish campaign, their losses too were high. Such was the sheer frustration of the crews of these light Panzers in the face of the heavier armoured French machines that some resorted to desperate expedients. One account speaks of a German Panzer commander attempting to climb on to a Hotchkiss H-35 with a hammer, presumably to smash the machine's periscopes, but falling off and being crushed by the tank's tracks. Certainly by day's end, Prioux had reason to claim that his tanks

An SdKfz 223 radio car fords the River Ourthe beside a destroyed bridge on 22 May 1940.

had come off best. The battlefield around Hannut was littered with the knocked out and destroyed tanks – the bulk of which were German Panzers – with by far and away the bulk of them being *Panzer* Is and IIs.

On day two of the battle, Hoeppner concentrated his two Panzer Divisions to form a *schwerpunkt* directed at the positions held by 3rd Light Mechanised Division and broke through the enemy line, thereby by-passing the 2nd Mechanised Division which was left 'out on a limb' by the German manoeuvre. In consequence, the manner in which all the French armour had been deployed in the long line so beloved of French military doctrine, meant that there was no reserve force to hand with which they could counter-attack the enemy breakthrough. Prioux therefore had no choice but to pull all of his forces back 'as a piece' towards the Gembloux Gap, to re-establish a contiguous line with the forces already guarding that position. Even so, the diary of *Panzer* Regiment 35 of 4. *Panzer Division* noted that the French had inflicted heavy casualties and that continuation of the battle would have been tantamount to 'suicide'. The final reckoning of this two-day encounter, despite German attempts to suggest otherwise, went in favour of the French. On a straight tank versus tank loss basis, the French lost 105 machines of which 30 were Somuas. German losses were much higher, with as many as 160 Panzers being lost. Nonetheless, most of the surviving French armour was able to pull back behind the Dyle line, and more importantly, Prioux had done as ordered and delayed the German advance. There, however, Prioux had the disheartening experience of senior officers pulling rank on him and dismembering the remnants of his formation. His tank battalions were dispersed along the line and amid the infantry formations.

There was, however, more to this encounter than a simple clash of armour. It was also the first time that two utterly contrasting doctrines of how armour should operate were tested in the arena of combat. The Panzer crews noted many of the limitations inherent in the design of French tanks which affected their combat effectiveness. It was also felt that they were operated in a 'leaderless, aimless, badly commanded' and 'tactically inferior' way. Nor could they effectively contend with an enemy that fought with combined arms, one of which was the crucial support of the *Luftwaffe* which provided close support with Stukas and Hs 123s. However, this only lasted through to midday on the 13th, when the *Luftwaffe* units were shifted south to help in the aerial assault on Sedan.

SIEG IM WESTEN

KFZ13
Weight: 2.2 tonnes
Crew: 3
Engines: Adler Standard 6, 12/50 HP
Speed: 30 km/h
Armament: 1 x 7.92mm MG 13
Length: 4.20 m
Width: 1.70 m
Height: 1.5 m
Armour: 8mm

A KFZ13 showing signs of wear as a result of the French campaign. The colour plate depicts a vehicle from an unknown unit as it would have appeared prior to receiving the damage, with grey and brown camouflage broken only by a narrow-armed white cross filled in with black.

© COPYRIGHT HILARY LOUIS DOYLE

Pz IIIs Ausf E and other vehicles of 1 PzDiv approaching the River Maas crossing in Holland, May 1940. The division sign can be seen on the Horch car's mudguard and on the turret front of the Pz III in the same photo as well as on the turret rears of the two Pz II, but the tanks' turret numbers are illegible.

SIEG IM WESTEN 41

A Pz IV Ausf B in Belgium during the invasion.

A Pz III Ausf F photographed in May 1940 at Palmersheim, in Germany near Bonn, ready for the invasion of France. The Ausf F can be distinguished from the Ausf E, far more common in the French campaign, by the armoured cowls added behind its headlights. Its only visible marking is the yellow inverted Y and dot of 5 PzDiv at the centre of the driver's front plate.

This shows the effect of artillery bombardment on a concrete bunker in Belgium. Although badly damaged it has not been penetrated by normal gunfire, showing why the pinpoint accuracy of the '88' was needed to 'post' shells through the gunports of such fortifications.

Hoeppner ordered his two Panzer Divisions to follow up the retreating French who were pulling back to the Gembloux Gap. In some cases, German Panzers found themselves caught up amid retreating French units. Hoeppner wished to take advantage of the confusion this would generate and hoped to be able to push through the Gembloux Gap and the Dyle line and do so before further French reinforcements were brought forward to strengthen the position. On this occasion, the Germans were pulled up short. On the 14th, he ordered 3. and 4. *Panzer* to make frontal attacks on the Allied line, but the Germans were rebuffed with heavy losses despite the provision of air support. The French forces had emplaced themselves behind a strong screen of anti-tank guns, which did the most damage to the oncoming German armour. The Panzers were also subjected to very heavy barrages from the 10 or 12 batteries of artillery located to the rear of the French positions.

The intensity of the fire from these batteries was likened by some of the Germans to the barrages of the First World War. In the face of such firepower Hoeppner called off the attack, in order to spare his two divisions any further heavy loss in casualties. However, unbeknown to him, infantry from 3. *Panzer Division* had forced their way into and through the French line, somewhat to the north of where the main tank assault had taken place and failed. Having broken up Prioux's command and allocated his armour in the manner laid down by the Service Regulations, the French now had no armoured reserve that could respond to this German incursion. With the line pierced in one place, the Germans were through the Gembloux defences.

The fighting of the previous four days had taken its toll on the strength of Hoeppner's two Panzer Divisions. By way of example, by daybreak on the 16th, 4. *Panzer* could only field 137 Panzers of the 314 it had on strength just six days before! Of the 177 'lost', not all were 'write-offs'. However, attrition was highest among the light Panzers and, given their very thin armour, more than a few of their crews had perished. Many of those tanks that had 'fallen out' were repairable, with the division reporting that 45 – 50 per cent of the Panzers were not as of that day ready for combat.

The 15th brought the news of the Dutch surrender. 9. *Panzer Division*, as the sole armoured formation allocated to the invasion of Holland, had had a relatively 'easy' war thus far. As the Dutch had no armour of their own, save for a small number of heavy armoured cars, the principal difficulty facing the tanks of this formation was in coping with the many water obstacles that lay astride their route of advance into Holland. By the 13th, 9. *Panzer* had reached the Moerdjik estuary. The only encounter between French armour and 9. *Panzer* on this part of the front saw the Germans come off second best. With the Dutch surrender, von Bock was told to release all of his armoured divisions so they could be allocated to strengthen the thrust by Army Group A across northern France.

These Pz 38(t) Ausf B are seen attacking a French position behind a boundary wall. Breaches in the wall have been made by the defenders for their heavy weapons, but these seem confined to machine guns – if anti-tank guns were present, the tanks should be spread more widely. The typical large red turret numbers with white outlines used by 7. PzDiv can be seen and so the unit here must be either PzRegt 25 or PzAbt 66. Even in this colour photograph, the contrast between the grey and brown camouflage is indistinct, but brown can be seen on the engine deck of the tank in the right foreground.

The Advance through the Ardennes

IT had been suspected, once the final form of *Gelb* had been settled, that the initial difficulty with which the forces of Army Group A would have to contend would be that of traffic congestion. So it proved. The first of von Rundstedt's forty-five divisions crossed the Luxembourg frontier at 0535 hrs on 10 May and began the push through the Ardennes. However, on the opening day of the offensive, only Guderian's XIX. *Panzerkorps* actually succeeded in crossing the border and moving westward. Traffic chaos was overwhelming under a sky of azure blue. *Panzerkorps Reinhardt*, consisting of 6. and 8. *Panzer Divisions*, was not only still on German soil by day's end but, along with the Motorised Corps *Wietersheim,* was still stuck to the east of the Rhine bridges!

This potential for traffic chaos had been seen early on in the war games conducted in April, which had addressed the thrust through the Ardennes. Difficulty was bound to arise given the vast number of vehicles that would be attempting to make passage on the few roads through the region. The five divisions of *Panzergruppe Kleist* alone were deploying 1,222 tanks, 545 half-track prime movers and 39,333 lorries and other vehicles transporting ammunition, food, spare parts and POL (Petrol, Oil and Lubricants). To this were added the immense number of other vehicles, horse drawn wagons, artillery units and marching infantry divisions clogging up the roads as they too began their advance to the west. On the 12th, traffic jams extended for some 250 kilometres from the northern part of the Army Group A's sector all the way back to the Rhine. Frieser describes the problems facing Reinhardt's command in detail – it serving as an illustrative example of the general traffic chaos in this sector of the front. He relates how on 12 May:

' ..there was from time to time a complete breakdown of march movement traffic on the right wing. A hopeless mess developed because vehicle convoys of the infantry divisions repeatedly forced their way out of the right-hand neighbour's combat sector into the wider roads that were aside for the Panzer Divisions. The infantry units acted like rivals of the Panzer units and did not want them to have all the glory. That resulted in jumbled confusion on the Ardennes trails, which turned out to be worse than the disaster scenario that Reinhardt had painted earlier in his war games as a kind of devil's advocate. Instead of immediately being able to start the race to the Meuse with Guderian's Panzers as had been planned, his units were caught up in a traffic jam for two days on German soil. The first vehicle of Reinhardt's 6. *Panzer Division* crossed the Luxembourg boundary only on the third day, at 0600 on 12 May'.

Given the clarity of the skies overhead and the relative dearth of *Luftwaffe* cover – most air assets being involved further north in support of Army Group B – the oft-used word 'miracle' does not seem out of place given the unprecedented target such traffic jams provided for Allied aircraft. Yet they did not come. Why not? It was not as if Gamelin was in ignorance that the Germans were making passage through the Ardennes. On the 11th, intelligence had been forwarded that German tanks had been spotted in some numbers advancing through the 'impassable' expanse of the forest. This was, however, explained away thus: 'the principal enemy effort seems to concern the region between Maastricht and Nijmegen: a reasonably violent *secondary* (author italics) effort is in progress west of Luxembourg'. When on the following day yet more reports flowed in, they too were accounted for in a manner which served to reinforce these French expectations. No amount

PANZERWAFFE

Divisional strengths for Panzer Divisions with Army Group A (von Rundstedt) – 10 May 1940

Division	Pz 1	Pz II	Pz III	Pz IV	Pz.35(t)	Pz.38(t)	Pz.Bef	Totals	Korps
1. Pz		52	98	58	40		8	256	**XIX. Panzerkorps** Guderian
2. Pz	45	115	58	32			16	250	
10. Pz	44	113	58	32			18	265	
6. Pz		60		31	118		14	223	**XLI. Panzerkorps** Reinhardt
8. Pz		58		23		116	15	212	
5. Pz	97	120	52	32			26	327	**XV. Panzerkorps** Hoth
7. Pz	34	68		24		91	8	225	

These Pz IV Ausf D are clearly breaking through the same wall that the Pz 38(s) seen on page 41 were attacking and so must also belong to 7. PzDiv. Brown and grey camouflage can be seen, as can the rust on their exhaust silencers, but the markings clearly seen on the foreground tank are unusual. Its turret side bears a red 321 with white outline but the turret rear has only the 32 without the 1, repeated on each side of its curve in red with a pale grey outline, and a central black and white cross on the bulge under the commander's cupola.

Here another Pz IV Ausf D demonstrates the use of its 7.5 cm gun to fire high-explosive shells against the same French position. It has a black-and-white cross with thicker arms in the same position but the dust raised by the shot makes it impossible to see any other markings.

A Pz II Ausf A or B of PzRegt 8, 10 PzDiv, approaches a bridge over the River Meuse near Sedan during the invasion of France. No tactical number is visible but the Roman II identifies it as from the 2nd company and the regimental wolfsangel confirms its unit identity. The Nazi flag stretched over its engine deck for air identification almost completely covers the white rectangle ordered for that purpose.

of evidence could disturb the intransigent mindset which categorically insisted that the main German offensive effort was at that moment fully underway in central Belgium. This serves as a most remarkable demonstration of the truth of the biblical expression: 'that there are none as blind as them that cannot see'! The problem for the French would be that, by the time the scales fell from their eyes, the Germans would be across the Meuse and defeat would be staring them in the face.

The Germans surmounted the many obstacles that they encountered as they made passage across the Ardennes – both manmade and natural. In the north, Hoth was making rapid progress towards the Meuse with Rommel's 7. *Panzer* in the van. Even Reinhardt's *Korps* had managed to extricate itself from the traffic jams and at last make good time towards the west. Further south, Guderian's *Panzerkorps* was doing likewise, his men constantly reminded of the need for ever greater speed. Here, 1. *Panzer Division* was taking the lead. Guderian had repeatedly stated to the men of this formation in the weeks leading up to the start of the offensive and in a manner that had led to his words acquiring the status of a mantra: 'In three days to the Meuse, on the fourth day across the Meuse'. In the service of this demand, he expected them to advance regardless of their lack of sleep. Time was of the absolute essence! To ward off their inevitable fatigue, his tank crews had been issued with *panzerchokolade* – soldiers slang for an early amphetamine called Pervetin. A great many were 'popped' during this period.

The French forces deployed in the Ardennes – albeit only some kilometres east of the Meuse – were tasked with setting up a defence line that was to all intents a trip wire. As we have seen, there was absolutely no expectation of a massive German thrust through the Ardennes directed at Sedan. If any enemy force did come through the Ardennes, the High Command's presumption was that its role was *diversionary* and that its intention would be to move south-west with a view to wheeling behind the Maginot Line. It was for this reason that Ninth Army, deployed along a line running below Namur southward through to Sedan, and which lay directly astride Army Group A's thrust line, had not been well equipped – either in the quality of its soldiery or armour. There was then a remarkable inconsistency between the task it had been given – to delay the approach of an enemy before falling back on the Meuse line – and the wherewithal provided to execute that role.

Events had not augured well for the Allies, when on 10 May, Belgian forces whom the French had presumed would assist in the defence – the fabled *Chasseurs Ardennais* – were unilaterally pulled out and sent north, thus severely weakening Ninth Army's defensive screen from the outset. Although there were demolitions of small bridges, mines placed in roads and so on, these were at best fitful attempts to oppose the Germans and the French forces pulled back toward the Meuse in the face of the German pressure. Their ability to resist was also impaired by their slavish adherence to contiguous lines. When the Ninth Army's forces defending the approaches to Sedan could not effect a link in the south with those of Second Army, the coherence of their front disintegrated, and the units were pulled back across the river before the end of the 12th.

The Germans had made passage through the Ardennes even more quickly than they had expected. Of the arrival of Hoth's Panzers on the Meuse, von Bock penned the following in his diary:

'Concerning Army Group A, the 4th Army has succeeded in crossing the Meuse near Yvoir and Dinant and has established bridgeheads there. The French really do seem to have taken leave of their senses….'

The next three days would demonstrate how true his words were.

PANZERWAFFE

Here we have the relatively rare opportunity to see photographs taken from front and rear of the same tank on a single occasion. The Pz I Ausf B is itself unusual, being one of a short series of Ausf B chassis built without superstructures or turrets but with armoured engine decks instead of thin sheet steel and with the electrical equipment of a normal Ausf B. These were known as Umsetz-Fahrzeuge (convertible vehicles) and were intended for use as driver training tanks that could be fitted with the superstructures and turrets of Ausf A tanks which were no longer battle-worthy. Only 147 were built, and it is not known how many were actually converted, but this is one of them as shown by the position of the lifting hooks on its turret – the Ausf A hooks were on the turret sides, those of the Ausf B on the turret top. It bears the 'sideways E' of 3 PzDiv in yellow at front and rear, with wide-armed white outline crosses on sides and rear. It also has the personal marking of an Iron Cross on its turret rear with the date 5.6.40 below it in white and a crewman's name split to its sides, also in white. Such markings usually commemorate the death of a crewman, but this one might instead record the award of an Iron Cross decoration. Unfortunately, the name is not fully legible but every endeavour has been made to reconstruct it for this colour plate.

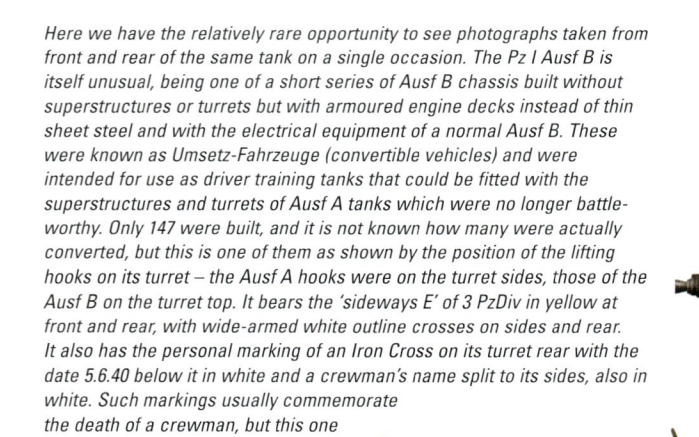

© COPYRIGHT HILARY LOUIS DOYLE

Panzerkampfwagen 1 B

Weight: 5.8 tonnes
Crew: 2
Engine: Maybach NL 38 TR, 100 HP
Speed: 40 km/h
Armament: 2 x 7.92mm MG 13k
Length: 4.42 m
Width: 2.06 m
Height: 1.72 m
Armour: 8 to 15mm

© COPYRIGHT HILARY LOUIS DOYLE

© COPYRIGHT HILARY LOUIS DOYLE

A contemporary map (of a series) published in a German book in 1940 – 'Forward over the Battlefield' on the invasion of France. The map shows the German front line on the evening of 12 May. See Publisher's Note at the bottom of page two.

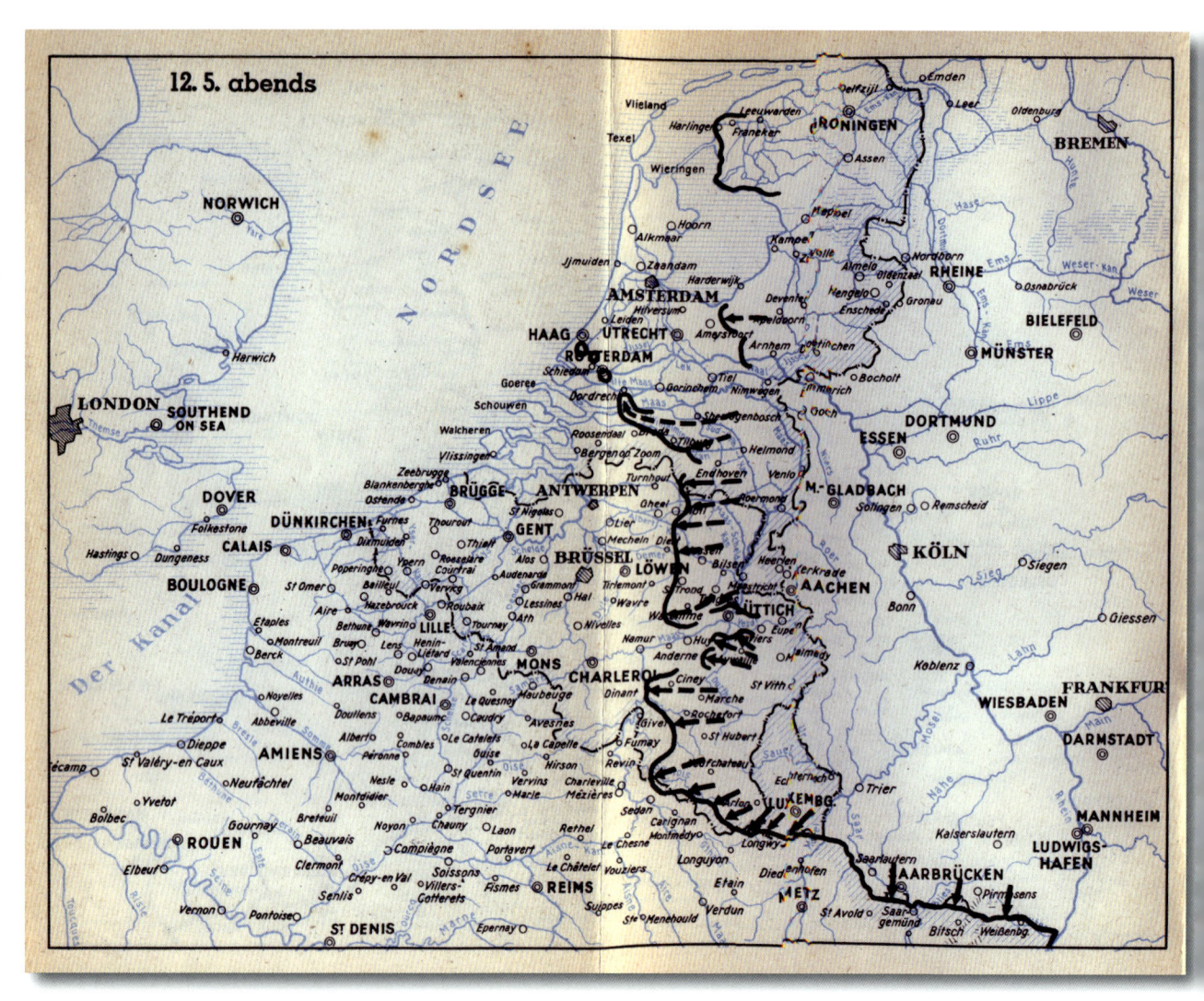

An SdKfz 221 or 223 – they cannot be told apart with the turret blown off – of 5 PzDiv is passed by marching infantry who look at it with interest.
The yellow division emblem of an inverted Y with two dots is on its frontplate below the white tactical sign for an armoured car unit, and it has the white G of a unit under Guderian's control on the driver's front plate and a white hollow cross on its rear side. Its registration number is WH-296334.

THE ADVANCE THROUGH THE ARDENNES

This Pz IV Ausf A belonged to 7 PzDiv whose yellow emblem can be seen on its superstructure side beside the white hollow cross. The divisions between the grey and brown of its camouflage can only just be seen. Unusually, its yellow turret number is split, with the large 6 on the side hatch and small 21 under the vision port ahead of it. The number of the Auf B beside it is not easy to read but appears to be 612. That tank has its division sign in the same place but carries a different style of cross.

A Pz III Ausf E in France shows its yellow tactical number 733 and white cross filled in with black on the back of its turret as well as the side. Its trackguards have done their job well, keeping the dust and dirt off the upper hull and turret so that the grey and brown camouflage can still be seen.

Here are two Pz I Ausf B and a Pz II Ausf a or b in the ruins of a French town. Their brown on grey camouflage can just be picked out. No division signs or tactical numbers are visible but the large white air recognition rectangle is clearly seen on the Pz II's engine deck. Under magnification, no change can be seen inside the central tank's Balkankreuz marking, so it seems that the cross on this tank was simply applied as a white outline over its grey and brown colours.

The Breakthrough at Sedan

IT was only on 14 May that the French High Command, so replete in the conviction that the main German assault was being directed at the Low Countries and the inevitable victory that would flow from it, came to the appalling realisation, that they had been duped. Rather, it would appear, the true gravity of the enemy's primary offensive effort lay elsewhere. Although Gamelin and his colleagues had, as we have seen, been in receipt of evidence of a German thrust through the Ardennes for the previous three days, its importance had never registered as anything more than 'a diversionary effort'. It could not have been otherwise in their eyes, for the notion that it was anything else flew in the face of the rigid preconceptions upon which the whole of their strategy was based. The dawning realisation that they had been totally wrong-footed by Germany's true strategy was first conveyed in a message from *General* Henri Lacaille, chief of staff of the French Second Army, in one of History's great understatements: 'There has been a rather serious hitch at Sedan'.

By day's end on 12 May, all three *Panzerkorps* of Army Group A had arrived at the Meuse along a front of some seventy kilometres. In the north Hoth's command, 5. and 7. *Panzer Divisions*, had arrived near Dinant. Reinhardt's three Panzer Divisions were at Montherme, albeit arriving only as night fell. Further to the south, Guderian's XIX. *Panzerkorps* rolled into a Sedan that was described as 'completely dead and still. Not a cat or dog did I see in the streets'. Lady Luck had certainly seen fit to dispense her favours to the Germans as their forces advanced through the Ardennes without having to face real opposition. Her largesse did not extend, however, to granting the boon of an easy passage across the Meuse. In consequence of their rapid pull back to the west bank of the river, the French had blown up all of the bridges. The Germans would now have no choice but to put to good use the pontoons that had been transported with such difficulty along the narrow and winding roads of the Ardennes. They were faced with executing one of the most difficult of all military operations – the forcing of a river crossing in the face of heavy enemy fire followed thereafter by the construction of a number of pontoon bridges. It was at Sedan, during the following three days, that the great drama of the French campaign would be played out.

For the French Army, now ensconced in its defences on the western bank of the river, there seemed to be little reason to be immediately concerned. Indeed, their quiescence and passivity was explicable in terms of their assumption that, in the absence of the large quantities of heavy artillery that would be necessary to blanket the French defences, the Germans could attempt no crossing. By the logic of the Great War, this was true. As the bulk of Army Group A's heavy guns were still making their slow horse-drawn passage through the Ardennes, it would be at least another week before they could arrive at Sedan. By then French reinforcements would have arrived to bolster a defensive system running along the west bank of the Meuse that was believed by them to be impregnable.

On paper there seemed to be every reason to support such a view. The Meuse line at Sedan was heavily fortified and six kilometres deep. It consisted of 103 bunkers, so constructed as to provide interlocking fire. These were, in turn, supported by artillery casemates with 75mm guns which commanded superb views across the river and its valley. To the rear of the main belt were fixed heavy artillery positions with guns that

A Pz IV Ausf B advances along a crowded road in France. The turret crew have obviously decided that hanging out of their side hatches is uncomfortable, though one might not think that sitting on the open hull hatches was any better. Since the tank is moving, the driver must be in his usual position looking through his visor, though what he thought of having his fresh air blocked by the gunner's leg can only be guessed at.

could easily target the river, any potential crossing points and the town of Sedan itself. However, the older bunkers were in a state of disrepair whilst many others were still under construction. Those actually in use were manned by troops of the 147th Infantry Division. These were first-line soldiers. However, the deeper positions were manned by troops of the 55th Infantry Division, a grade 'B' reserve formation, neither as well trained nor as well armed as the 147th. The first reinforcement arrived on the morning of 13 May, when the 71st Infantry Division was deployed at Sedan.

By the logic of the previous generation, the French assumption about artillery was correct. However, Guderian, who had always intended that Sedan would be the decisive crossing point along the Meuse, had no intention of waiting for more artillery. Not only would he make do with those pieces already to hand in the artillery units of his Panzer Divisions, but he had made provision in advance for what was still, at the time, a novel substitute. He would use the *Luftwaffe*. Although after the campaign *Generalmajor* Wolfram *Freiherr* von Richthofen would repudiate the notion that the sole purpose of the German air arm's existence was to provide support for ground operations, by colourfully stating that the '*Luftwaffe* was not the *Heer*'s whore', on this occasion it seemed more than happy to service the Army's needs!

It had always been planned that, once the Allied forces had been drawn *en masse* into Belgium, the bulk of *Luftwaffe* assets, which had for the first four days been operating almost exclusively in support of Army Group B's operations there and in Holland, would be transferred to support the operations of Army Group A. Although fewer air assets than were originally planned for were subsequently used at Sedan, the massive aerial assault on the French defences would nevertheless amount to the heaviest sustained attack on such a narrow front ever executed by the *Luftwaffe* during World War Two. Most of the committed *Luftwaffe* assets came from *Luftflotte* III. It had been planned that the greatest concentration of bombing would be on those sectors of the Meuse loop that were the designated crossing points for the assault teams of the three Panzer Divisions. Upstream was 10. *Panzer*, with its crossing point designated at Wadelincourt. Downstream lay 2. *Panzer*, which was scheduled to cross over at Donchery. However, the primary thrust would be undertaken by 1. *Panzer* at Gaulier, in the centre. It was, however, the stretch from Gaulier running through to 10. *Panzer*'s sector which was scheduled to receive the greatest attention from the *Luftwaffe*. It was also directly across from the designated primary crossing point at Gaulier that Guderian stationed the bulk of the artillery available to his three divisions. Even so, their paucity of ammunition precluded a sustained or heavy barrage and, according to witnesses, the contribution of the German artillery seems to have been lost against the backdrop of the bombing, once it began.

This attack began at 0800 hrs on the 13th with no fewer than 1,500 aircraft detailed to participate in a series of rolling raids which were scheduled to last the better part of eleven hours – through to dusk. During the course of these raids no fewer than 1,215 sorties flown by He 111s, Do 17, Ju 88s and Stukas were directed at just the four-kilometre section of the Meuse Loop between Gaulier and Wadelincourt. The crescendo arrived at 1540 when a massive raid by 750 medium and dive-bombers arrived to saturate this area through to 1600 hrs, when the assault boats carrying infantry and combat engineers began to cross the river.

The expectation that the massive scale of this aerial assault would have demolished the defences was not met. It was later ascertained that the actual material damage was slight and that the real effect on the defenders – albeit not all of them – was psychological. Testimony to this would be provided by the survivors of 10. *Panzer's* team, who had eighty-one out of their ninety-six assault boats sunk by machine gun fire directed from the bunkers. The survivors who landed then formed the basis of the divisional bridgehead. The more open aspect of the terrain in 2. *Panzer Division's* sector permitted the French to call down accurate and heavy fire, which prevented the assault team from even getting into the water at the appointed time for their crossing. It was only some hours after the other two divisions that 2. *Panzer* managed to get a small force across the river.

It was in the centre that the greatest success was achieved, when infantry and assault engineers from the elite *Grossdeutschland* regiment, which had been attached to 1. *Panzer* for the duration of the campaign, managed to locate a gap in the enemy defences. Their rapid infiltration of the defensive zone was aided by their discovery that the positions in the rear held by the reserve troops of the 55th Infantry Division had been abandoned when panic had set in during the course of the bombing raids. Pushing forward into a virtual vacuum, the 1st Rifle Regiment pushed forward eight kilometres into the French defences. Unbeknown to the Germans, the impact of the bombing had done more than just panic those troops of the 55th Infantry Division to the rear of the bunker line. As they fled, the panic spread like a contagion. Troops manning the rearward artillery batteries abandoned their guns while, ten kilometres to the rear, a rumour that German tanks were already in the French positions had led to a mass desertion of the important Bulson Ridge.

Clearing the enemy in this sector of the defensive zone had enabled engineer troops to begin the rapid assembly of a pontoon bridge at Gaulier. As early as 1910 hrs ferry had been assembled and proceeded to take across 37mm Pak and 75mm light infantry guns to provide fire support for the troops advancing inland from the river, in addition to infantry reinforcements. Although the pontoon bridge itself was finished by 0100 hrs, there were no Panzers at hand to cross the river until over six hours later. At 0300 hrs, three armoured reconnaissance patrols, consisting of four-wheeled Sdkz 222 and eight-wheeled SdKfz 232 and SdKfz 264 armoured cars, crossed over to the west bank. Thus when the first French reports filtered back to Vincennes reporting the presence of German tanks on the west side of the river, they were in error as it was only at 0720 hrs that the first Panzers began to cross the river. Prior to that, armoured cars, lorries, half-tracks and other traffic, but certainly not armour, were moving across the bridge in strength. At the time of the bridge's completion, the tanks of 1. *Panzer* were in laager some 16 kilometres from the river, and although they were put on alert to move out as early as 0120 hrs, it took until 0720 for the first tanks to make it on to the bridge. By then the roads feeding on to the river frontage and the bridge were filled with traffic. This in turn became the target for surviving French artillery which proceeded to shell the queues. Periodically the air was rent by a detonation as a vehicle was hit and black smoke plumes rose above the town on the east bank.

By the early hours of the 14th, it was becoming clear to the French that something exceedingly serious was happening at Sedan. Although they had not yet divined the enemy's true strategic intent, it was enough for them to appreciate that the bridge at Gaulier, and the one established at Wadelincourt by 10. *Panzer* which came on line later in the morning, represented a danger of the gravest order. In little over twelve hours the 'hitch at Sedan', had transmuted itself in their consciousness into something altogether more threatening. The full measure of the growing French anxiety over what was happening there is revealed in the apocalyptic words of General Billotte when speaking to the commander of the French Air Force in the northern operations zone. He demanded all-out effort by the Allied air forces: ' *La victorie ou la défaite passent par ces ponts*' – 'victory or defeat will depend on these bridges'.

However, the corollary was also true. For the Germans the fate of *Fall Gelb* now stood or fell on the fate of these bridges. Although Hitler had waxed lyrical about the success achieved thus far, describing the crossing of the Meuse as 'a miracle, an absolute miracle', divine intervention had absolutely nothing to do with it. Guderian understood as much as did the French what the crossing point at Gaulier represented.

A Pz IV Ausf A and an uparmoured Pz II Ausf A or B in a French town. The Pz II has the white tactical number 301 and a hollow white cross, but the crewmen standing around conceal any markings on the Pz IV.

PANZERWAFFE

THE BREAKTHROUGH AT SEDAN

Brueckenleger IVb
Weight: 28 tonnes approx
Crew: Probably 2
Engine: Maybach HL 120 TR, 265 HP
Speed: Unknown
Armament: None
Length: 9 m approx
Width: 3 m approx
Height: 3.6 m approx
Armour: 10 to 30mm

The Brueckenleger IVb bridgelayer is built on the chassis of a Pz IV Ausf D, and was used by PzPioBatt (Panzer Engineer Batallion) 39 of 3 PzDiv during the French campaign. It carries the tactical number 32 in red with white outlines on its sides and its port front and starboard rear mudflaps. The wide-armed white outline cross is painted directly over its grey and brown camouflage; it is repeated on the port rear mudflap and perhaps on the starboard front one as well, but that flap has been flipped up so any marking on it is not visible here.

Here two Pz IV Ausf A are seen still in service in France. The only visible markings are their white tactical numbers and the white hollow cross on the nearer tank.

Quite simply, if the French managed to destroy these structures then the bulk of the German forces on the east bank of the Meuse would be effectively isolated. Unable to get more bridging equipment in place quickly enough to maintain the offensive momentum which was the very basis of *Gelb*, even the ponderous French would have enough time in which to redeploy their powerful forces from Belgium and block any further attempt by Army Group A to advance into France. In effect, the German offensive would then wither 'on the vine'. Herein lays the nature of Halder's acceptance of *Gelb* being an all or nothing plan. Either the Germans succeeded in this incredibly risky venture, or the war would be lost in 1940. For both France and Germany, all now stood on the fate of those two bridges.

THE AIR ASSAULT ON THE BRIDGES AT SEDAN

Guderian had understood this even before the actual launch of the German offensive and had made full provision both for the air and ground defence of them. In terms of the latter, he had assembled the most formidable collection of anti-aircraft guns yet seen. The core of the ground defences was built around the 102nd Flak Regiment with its 88mm, 37mm and 20mm weapons, to which were added the 20mm light Flak weapons of the three respective Panzer Divisions for a grand total of 303 Flak guns. The need to ensure that the bridges were protected on both sides of the river had seen many of these weapons making early passage across to the west bank before dawn. The defensive shield around the bridges was in place early on the 14th in anticipation of a major assault by the Allied air forces to destroy them. Overhead, the *Luftwaffe* had provided a large number of Bf 109s to provide an aerial umbrella.

Given the extreme danger posed at Sedan, it is surprising that the Allies could only manage to assemble a strike force of a mere 152 bombers and 250 fighters. By day's end, the French and British survivors had coined the expression 'the furnace over Sedan' as a way of describing the experience of running the gauntlet of the Bf 109s and then flying through the hail of fire from the Flak guns around the targets. Freiser recounts the following about the Allied air attacks:

'A single bomb hit on the Gaulier bridge would have sufficed to jeopardize the success of the operation where 'every minute counted'. On 14 May, Guderian kept driving to Gaulier over and over again and, to make a statement, positioned himself on the bridge to set an example to his soldiers. After all, on that day there was no more dangerous place in all of France than that bridge. Around noon even von Rundstedt, the commander of Army Group A, showed up. Guderian made his report to him in the middle of the bridge. Precisely at that moment, enemy aircraft attacked the bridge so that both generals had to seek cover. Then Rundstedt asked 'Is it always like this here?' As Guderian noted in his *Memoirs*, he was able to answer this question 'with a clear conscience, that it was.'

Another mechanised unit with SdKfz 11s and leFH18s passes through a wrecked French town in May 1940. The letter G on the half-track is not the gun letter but the designator for units under the command of General Guderian.

A Pz IV Ausf C advancing along a French road carries the white oakleaf sign of 1 PzDiv on its turret front. The spare wheel on its side is accompanied by a log roll for laying on soft ground to stop the tank sinking in.

PANZERWAFFE

A Pz I Ausf B of 5 PzDiv, whose yellow sign is barely visible beside the hollow white cross. The turret number and the bar below it also appear to be yellow. The figure 208 chalked on its hull rear is unexplained, but the divisions of its grey and brown camouflage are faintly visible.

An 8.8 cm 'bunkerknacker' is towed round a road corner in France. Its armoured half-track bears on its front mudguard the tactical sign for a towed heavy anti-tank unit, but unfortunately the battalion number beside it is illegible.

These two views of the towed 'bunkerknacker' 8.8 cm show that they were repainted in the grey and brown colour scheme for the invasion of France. Once again an unarmoured half-track is being used to tow the gun.

All told, by day's end the Allies had lost 114 bombers – by far the greater number of these belonging to the RAF. Both air arms lost 167 aircraft in total. For the *Jagdflieger* of II. *Fliegerkorps,* such was the scale of their success that 14 May was known thereafter as the 'Day of the Fighters'. By day's end on the 14th the bridges were still in place and, more importantly, by dusk over 600 Panzers had crossed the river. These included those of 2. *Panzer Division*, which Guderian had ordered across the Gaulier bridge in lieu of using their own, which had not yet been completed.

THE TANK BATTLE AT BULSON

The seven hour delay in getting Panzers across the river between 0120 and 0730 hrs could have been potentially disastrous for the Germans, as the French had already organised a counter-attack on the bridgehead with tanks and infantry. Although ordered in the afternoon of the previous day, delays, procrastination and, not least, the impact of the confusion generated by the panic during the night, saw the French attack only begin early on the 14th. Departing from their start line at 0730 hrs, the French force made for the Bulson Ridge with a view to ensuring that the site, having been vacated in the night by panicked infantry, would once more be secured. Ultimately, however, the objective was to destroy the German bridgeheads. While that may have been realisable the day before, the odds were no longer stacked in the French favour.

These Pz IV seen in France are either Ausf B or C, identifiable by their lack of the plain drum cupola of the Ausf A and use of the early-type tracks with low guide horns as seen carried on their engine decks. The differences between B and C are only visible from the front. They have been fitted with turret-rear stowage bins made by their unit, but bear no visible division emblem.

Given the short distance the French needed to traverse before reaching their initial objective, their speed was dilatory. That being said, the forty FCM-36 tanks were classed as infantry support machines. One of the rarer beasts in the French armoured inventory – just one hundred had been built, with production curtailed early because of its high unit price – the FCM had a top speed of only 24 kph. Given that French military doctrine required this class of tank to advance no faster than the foot soldiers it was there to support, it is not surprising that it was not thought necessary to design it to go faster. It thus took until 0845 for the French force to cover the two kilometres to Bulson, where they were pipped at the post by the first German tanks to have come across the Gaulier bridge which appeared before the French on the ridge, having travelled nine kilometres in less time. However, the lack of any plan to ensure that the more effective *Panzer* IIIs and IVs were given priority in crossing the bridge saw the initial clash of armour at Sedan involve mainly light Panzers supported by just a few of the mediums.

Although it was purely coincidental that the encounter at Bulson took place more or less at the same time as did the second day of the tank battle at Hannut and Merdorp in Belgium, in many ways the experiences of the Panzers in fighting French armour were the same. The experience of seeing 37mm shells fired from PaK36 anti-tank guns and the same calibre weapon in the *Panzer* III bouncing off the frontal armour of the French tanks certainly was the same. The initial encounter was not favourable to the Germans, with a number of their tanks being knocked out in rapid succession. Because of the need to hold the French at any cost, there was no finesse here in the deployment of the Panzers. As soon as the few there were arrived on the scene, they were sent into battle in the dribs and drabs fashion so derided by Guderian. But given the circumstances, even he acknowledged that *General* Kirchner had no other choice.

In the best fashion of a divisional Panzer commander, Kirchner had crossed early on in his command 251 SPW and, from his vantage point with its good view of the surrounding terrain, he was able to direct his arriving forces to where they were most needed. Here once again, we come to what was undoubtedly one of the most important aspects of Panzer warfare – the ability of these machines to move around and change direction because of orders issued over their onboard radios. The radios facilitated what Freiser meant when he stated:

THE BREAKTHROUGH AT SEDAN | **61**

This 'bunkerknacker' 8.8 cm seems to have lost its rear ammunition box. Perhaps it has been removed by the men seen on the vehicle while they carry out some maintenance jobs. The only markings on the grey and brown camouflage are its number plates, with even the usual cross missing from its side.

This self-propelled 'bunkerknacker' was knocked out in France. Here the gun-aimer's double handwheels are clearly seen; unlike the normal anti-aircraft gun, this version had both traverse and elevation wheels on the same side for rapid aiming by one man.

Here an armoured tractor tows a 'bunkerknacker' 8.8 cm across country.

'It was the speed with which the combat action took place that provided the most important difference between the two armies. The speed of the so-called command process – the time that passed between the realisation of a new situation, the response to it from the military leadership, and actual operations on the battlefield – played an essential role'.

This helped negate to a significant degree the design strengths of French armour. Furthermore, as at Hannut, it was found that the ability of German tanks to manoeuvre more rapidly by virtue of their higher speeds saw them able to close in on the FCMs and by-pass them. In the case of the *Panzer* IIIs and IVs this also permitted them to hit the French tanks in the flank – between the turret and the chassis – where the Panzer crews had discovered that French armour was vulnerable to penetration by their weapons.

Once again the light Panzers were revealed, in the words of one of the participating Panzer officers, to be 'unfit for combat'. In consequence they were deliberately kept back from the rolling encounter with the French tanks. However, during the course of the morning only four tank companies from 1. *Panzer Division* actually took part in this battle as the bulk of the division was still on the east bank waiting to cross by the time the French withdrew in the early afternoon. They left behind them almost all of their tanks. Other German weapons had also played their part in this clash. Notwithstanding the limitation of the Pak 36, anti-tank gunners persevered with their weapons, firing rapidly at the French tanks in order to secure a successful shot in one of the FCM's areas that were more vulnerable. Bulson marked the first ever combat use of the Stug III by *Grossdeutschland*'s assault gun battery. Also supporting the Panzers were Zgkw 12-ton half tracks mounting a modified 88mm Flak 18 and belonging to *schwere PanzerJägerAbteilung 8*, a unit seconded to 1. *Panzer Division* for the period of the campaign. It was noted how effectively the 88 penetrated the armour of the FCM.

The 14th May was possibly the most crucial day of the campaign. Although the French would make a further attempt to employ armour to strike at the southern flank of XIX. *Panzerkorps* in the days ahead, to all intents and purposes the 'writing was on the wall' for the Allied cause. In just five days, rampant optimism as to the successful outcome of the war had been replaced, as if overnight, by profound pessimism. It is abundantly clear that what the German breakthrough at Sedan presaged was nothing less than the defeat of France. That this was fully appreciated by the military and by the politicians in Paris is relayed by a number of accounts telling of senior French generals weeping over the news. Although a day later, the French Prime Minister Reynaud phoned his British counterpart. Churchill who was still abed, heard Reynaud say in English: 'We have been defeated!' In the momentary silence, Churchill grappled to come to

The crew of a towed 'bunkerknacker' 8.8 cm pose with their armoured half-track tractor. It is camouflaged in grey and brown, but like most of those vehicles it has no markings. An unarmoured half-track is behind it.

This is a Pz IV Ausf B of 9 PzDiv during the French campaign. Its tactical number 422 is carried in small yellow numbers at the top of the turret side and the Division's XX is beside the driver's visor.

64 PANZERWAFFE

A contemporary map (of a series) published in a German book in 1940 – 'Forward over the Battlefield' on the invasion of France. The map shows the German front line on the evening of 14 May. See Publisher's Note at the bottom of page two.

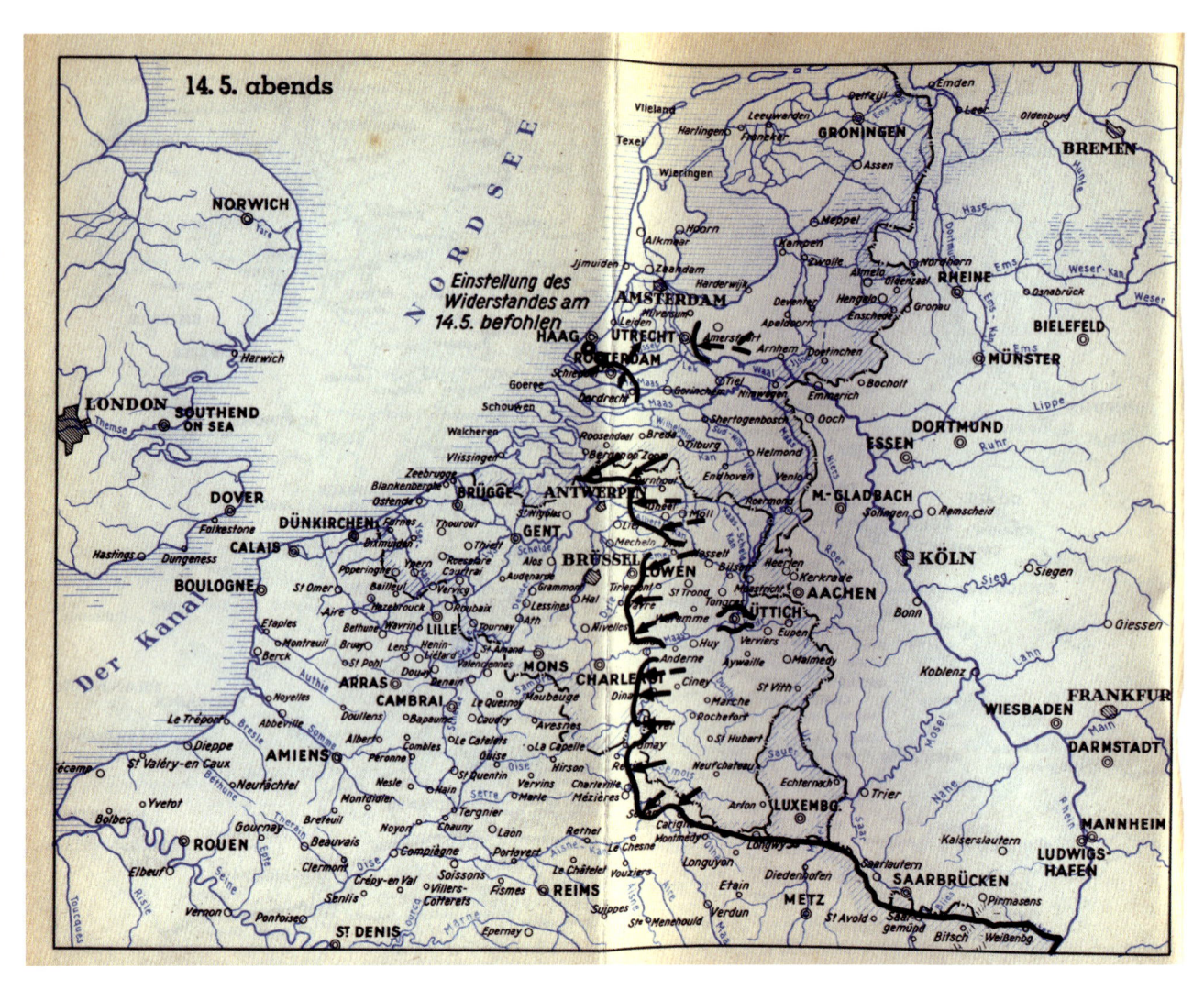

The crew of this Pz II Ausf b is relaxing after the capture of Sedan. The addition of a vertical plate to carry a front-facing cross is unusual but no division sign is visible and its turret number cannot be read in full.

THE BREAKTHROUGH AT SEDAN

This Pz I Ausf B shows the official Abwurfvorrichtung, noticeably different to the original version with reinforcements on its arms and a transverse frame to secure its support cable instead of a single pillar with the cable running through its top and secured to the superstructure rear. Two doors on the bottom of the armoured box at the end of the arms could be opened by another cable to let the explosive charge drop out on to an obstacle. It carries the yellow 'sideways E' of 3 PzDiv on its rear beside a hollow white cross and the partial name 'Wilhelm….' above an Iron Cross on its turret rear. Unfortunately, the rest of the name and its tactical number are unreadable though its grey and brown camouflage pattern can be seen in places.

In late 1939, an Abwurfvorrichtung (explosive charge dropping device) was developed by Pioneer-Battalion 38 of 2. PzDiv. It was fitted to Pz I tanks, and after proving successful, it was copied for official issue to the Panzer-Pioneers (armoured engineers) of every Panzer Division. This photograph shows a Pz I, apparently an Ausf A, with the two yellow dots of 2. PzDiv and displaying some of the details of the original device. It also carries an unusual cross for that period, with not just a black infill to its white arms but also a black outline to them in Luftwaffe style. In front of it is a Pz II Ausf B or C with tactical number 331 still shown on a rhomboid plate. It carries on its turret the white K of a unit assigned to Panzergruppe Kleist and an unknown tactical symbol. Ahead of them is a heavy car also with the K and showing the yellow dots of 2. PzDiv below the white rhomboid sign of a Panzer unit.

Not all relations with the locals were unfriendly. Here two Panzer crewmen chat with a woman who, if we are to judge by the name beside her door, may be of German descent.

This Pz II Ausf A or B and Pz 38(t) probably belong to 8 PzDiv. The grey and brown camouflage shows up clearly on the Pz II, which also carries the white air recognition rectangle on its engine deck. Its commander has stowed his steel helmet on the turret rear where he can reach it quickly, but the other crewmen have placed theirs on the starboard side of the superstructure – not very logical since they would exit the tank on its other side. Its exhaust is brown with rust, and the paint has rubbed off the wheels where the track's guidehorns rub against them. Both tanks have black crosses outlined in white.

Guderian unleashed
(or victory through insubordination)

This Pz II Ausf C in the French campaign shows the added armour that reinforced its turret front and its driver's front plate. It is unusual in having a machine gun mounted on a post on its turret top for anti-aircraft defence. It bears the two yellow dots denoting 2 PzDiv and the tactical number R02, still on the rhomboid plate used in 1939, of a tank from Regimental Headquarters. It is also unusual in bearing the white rhomboid 'Panzer unit' marking on its front with the regimental R as well as the division's two yellow dots; it was usually assumed that any tank must belong to a Panzer unit and so would not need the rhomboid. The white turret emblem appears to be a winged angel bearing a flaming torch; it is unidentified but may be the family heraldic badge of the tank's commander.

IT could be argued that the pivotal moment of the French campaign and in the history of the *Panzerwaffe* occurred in the early afternoon of the fifth day of *Fall Gelb* and turned on what was technically the insubordination of one man in the face of his superiors. For Heinz Guderian, self proclaimed and regarded Panzer prophet, his moment of destiny had come. For years he had been preaching to those 'too deaf to hear' about the war-winning potential implicit in the exploitation of success by fast moving, independent, concentrated armoured formations driving deep into the enemy's hinterland. At Sedan, his *Panzerkorps* had achieved an unprecedented success. Victory now turned on its exploitation.

In consequence, northern France now lay open to the Panzers and the Channel coast beckoned. Here was the opportunity to demonstrate, in the most dramatic fashion possible, that the intellectual convictions which had sustained him since the late 1920s concerning the primacy of armoured forces in war were grounded in reality and not the fantasy his critics had claimed. To do so, however, meant disobeying orders from Kleist through Von Rundstedt and Halder right up to the *Führer* himself, all of whom in one form or another had asserted that having breached the line of the Meuse, under no circumstances were the Panzers to advance further west. They were first to defend the bridgehead and await the arrival of the infantry that was on 14 May still making its passage through the Ardennes. For Guderian, this was tantamount to throwing away the victory achieved at Sedan. Above all, it would give the enemy time to recover from his shock and allow him to reorganise his still formidable forces. It might even permit the French to snatch victory from the jaws of defeat!

All of the above followed as he pondered the content of a radio message he had received at 1230 hrs. A reconnaissance unit of 1. *Panzer Division* had captured undamaged the bridge at Chemery, and was even now pushing further westward. Were they to continue? By doing so, this force had already gone beyond the halt line laid down by Kleist to Guderian. For an hour and a half he mulled over the issue. In the end, he asked the advice of his staff. He said his mind was made up when Walter Wenck (who in May 1945 was to command the army Hitler hoped would relieve Berlin), the operations officer of 1. *Panzer Division*, quoted back to Guderian one of his favourite aphorisms: *Klotzen, nicht kleckern!* Although these words allow to a number of translations, that of 'Hit with the fist, do not feel with the fingers' is probably the most apposite. For Guderian it was the decisive factor. He would go with his instincts even if it meant putting his career on the line. The order was issued that 1. and 2. *Panzer Divisions* would push westward 'towards Rethel', some forty kilometres from Sedan. The push for the Channel had begun.

The tank battle at Stonne

In the original plan formulated by Manstein with Guderian's advice, the primary Panzer thrust to the west and the Channel was intended to be screened by a feint attack directed at the south-east, as if the German intention was to turn the Maginot Line. Halder had eliminated this from the final plan for *Gelb* but, in another unilateral decision, Guderian gainsaid the Army Chief of Staff, and reinstated it. On 15 May, 10. *Panzer Division*, supported by the *Grossdeutschland* regiment, was ordered by him to strike south from the bridgehead, across the Stonne plateau.

It was here that the French were also marshalling their forces in preparation for a counter-attack on the bridgehead employing the *3e Division Cuirassée de Réserve*. The arrival of the German armour on the 15th, even as the French were preparing for their own attack, precipitated a significant armoured encounter between the two sides in and around the village of Stonne, which was to last the better part of two days and lead to the settlement changing hands on no fewer than seventeen occasions. Indeed, the battle for this innocuous village was to be the most vicious of the campaign. It also marked the only occasion when German armour came face to face with France's premier tank, in the form of the 32-ton Char B1-Bis, in any numbers. Inasmuch as Guderian had also seen this as a means of tying down the French until other units still crossing the Ardennes arrived in Sedan, it succeeded. The cost to the German forces in armour and manpower involved was high.

The first attempt to take the village resulted in the loss of seven Panzers, although it was in German hands by early morning. Between 0800 and 1045 hrs Stonne changed hands four times, in each case the Germans being ejected by French tanks. However, on each occasion they attacked alone but could not hold the village because of the lack of infantry support. The Germans thereupon returned. The Char B1 proved impregnable to the 37mm anti-tank guns. Once again the German gunners watched helplessly as their shells simply bounced off the armour of the 'monsters'. It was only after the Pak gunners had located a weak spot on the French tank's flank where the radiator grill was located, and fired well aimed shots, that they were able to bring them to a halt.

On the 16th, just one Char B1 broke through the German anti-tank defences and was able to knock out 13 Panzers and a number of anti-tank guns. The measure of the seeming invincibility of this machine was that in its turn it was the recipient of no less than 140 hits, of which not one penetrated its armour. On the following day there was a similar incident involving a solitary Char B1. The superiority of the French tank over its opponents was clear to see. However, in the absence of infantry support these singular operations could not carry the day for the French. Whilst they demonstrated the formidable nature of these machines, they were doomed to destruction as German tankers and Pak gunners gained the measure of their weaknesses.

By the time that 10. *Panzer* was relieved by the first of the follow-on infantry divisions on the 17th, thereafter joining 1. and 2. *Panzer* in the drive west, the French assaults had been contained. Stonne and its environs were described as a graveyard of gutted French and German armour. Photographs show blackened *Panzer* IIIs and IVs. Even though heavy fighting continued around Stonne through 17 May, by attacking when they had, 10. *Panzer* and *Grossdeutschland* had forestalled attempts by the French to organise themselves for their counter-attack. In the end, the French commander cancelled it. Although there were fitful attempts to revive it, it was all too late. Once more the French had been out-fought, not by a materially stronger enemy, but by combined arms and a flexibility and speed in operation that they could not match. Individual exploits of French bravery, and there were many at Stonne, could not compensate for an Army that was institutionally geared to the war-fighting methods of an earlier generation.

The drive for the Channel

At about midnight on 20 May, just six days after Guderian had given the green light to begin the advance westward from the Sedan bridgehead, a battalion of 2. *Panzer Division* reached the English Channel. With one cut of his tracked and motorised scythe, Guderian had severed the Allied forces in Belgium and northern

This SdKfz 251 Ausf A in France carries a very full set of markings. Under the yellow inverted Y of 1 PzDiv on one rear door is the white tactical sign for a motorised infantry unit with, beside it, a 1 for the first Kompanie. A white cross infilled with black is centred on both rear doors, and another is carried on the upper hull side. The half-track is fully stowed for the campaign, with various items slung over its back and its machine gun fitted to the rear mount. Modellers should note its radio aerial – not a thin whip but a tapering shaft. Since it carries the official Division emblem instead of the oak leaf, we can assume that the company commander was a 'stickler' for the regulations.

France, numbering over 1 million men, and all their equipment, from the rest of metropolitan France. Since the beginning of the thrust to the west six days before, Guderian and his two divisions, joined by 10. *Panzer* after the 17th, had faced little in the way of opposition from the French. What problems they did experience came from higher up their own chain of command. On a number of occasions Guderian had been called to task, and ordered to halt due to the timidity and fears of his superiors in the face of his extending and open flanks. Guderian was to write of this period: 'The High Command's influence on my actions has merely been restrictive throughout'. By inference, if given his head, his forces may have reached the Channel even earlier.

The first of these orders had occurred just one day after the advance had begun. That day had, unbeknown to the onrushing Panzers at the time, led to the destruction of the French rear line of defence and the last substantial enemy force between them and the Channel. On the evening of the 15th, the order came down from Kleist's headquarters to halt the advance. As before, Guderian was ordered to consolidate the bridgehead and await the arrival of the infantry. Again, he bridled. In a heated exchange with Kleist over the telephone, he demanded that he be permitted to resume the advance. Kleist relented, permitting Guderian to resume the advance so as to 'widen the bridgehead sufficiently for us to allow the infantry corps to follow us' – a form of words sufficiently ambiguous as to permit the advance to resume, but also protect the *Panzergruppe* commander from any recrimination from above should things go awry.

On the 16th, von Rundstedt developed 'cold feet'. The ever-nagging fear that the rapidly extending flanks of the advancing Panzer Divisions were just crying out to be attacked by the Allies had by now become overwhelming: 'the enemy is in no circumstances to be allowed to achieve any kind of success, even if only a local success'. A stop line was then placed on the Panzers. Only 'advanced units' could pass beyond the line Beaumont-Hirson-Montcornet-Gruignicourt. They, too, were restricted to moving no further than 48 kilometres beyond that. The risks in permitting the Panzer Divisions to plunge headlong further west 'could not be justified'. These words merely echoed Hitler's sentiments for it was he who had voiced these concerns when visiting Army Group A's headquarters earlier that day. It was also he who demanded the halt order, mesmerised as he was by the inevitability of a non-existent threat to the southern flank. That same evening von Brauchitsch gave OKH's blessing to Army Group A's halt order.

The 15 cm schwere Infanteriegeschuetz 33 auf Fahrgestell Panzer I (15 cm heavy infantry cannon on Panzer I chassis), sIG 33 sfl auf Pz I for short, is more conveniently known as the Bison I. This one is gun B of sIGKompanie 703, serving with 2 PzDiv in France in May/June 1940. The name Bismarck has been painted below the gun and the gun letter B is carried on the bulge of the side below the German cross. Bismarck's front trackguard extensions have been removed to prevent the build-up of mud under them but gun Edith, in the background, still has them mounted.

Kleist flew in early the following morning to give Guderian the news personally. He wanted no ambiguity in the passing on of this order! Guderian was incredulous. 'After the wonderful success of 16 May, it did not occur to me that my superiors might still be thinking on the same lines as before'… The ferocious argument that now broke out between the two men culminated in Guderian proffering Kleist his resignation, which the latter accepted. However, his relief was temporary and later in the day General List appeared at Guderian's HQ and reinstated him. An olive branch was held out. List gave Guderian the green light to send forward 'strong reconnaissance' forces, on the proviso that his Corps HQ would remain at Montcornet. Never one to take an inch when he could take a mile, Guderian resumed the advance but ran a telephone line back to his HQ, which stayed put as ordered. However, this halt order had cost him two days. Although in that time the tank crews gained some much-needed rest and also were able to attend to the maintenance of their charges, the opportunity had been lost to take advantage of a virtual collapse in the French front.

Hitler's halt order had been grounded on trepidation and fear; his obsession with the southern flank was irrational. There was no threat. Halder stated that the Army knew from the extensive reconnaissance sorties flown by the *Luftwaffe* that the French had no significant forces to hand with which to mount even a limited attack. Even so, it led to heated exchanges between the leader and Halder. Hitler would have none of it. He knew best, and the military acquiesced in a decision they knew to be wrong. It would set the precedent for the future.

Essential in aiding Guderian's drive to the coast was the very close air support provided by the dive-bombers of *Fliegerkorps VIII* under the command of von Richthofen. Moving with the spearhead were

This Pz III Ausf E has just smashed through a rudimentary road block in France. A BefPz I waits behind the remaining stones to follow it.

PANZERWAFFE

A contemporary map (of a series) published in a German book in 1940 – 'Forward over the Battlefield' on the invasion of France. The map shows the German front line on the evening of 2 June – observe the German line around Dunkirk. See Publisher's Note at the bottom of page two.

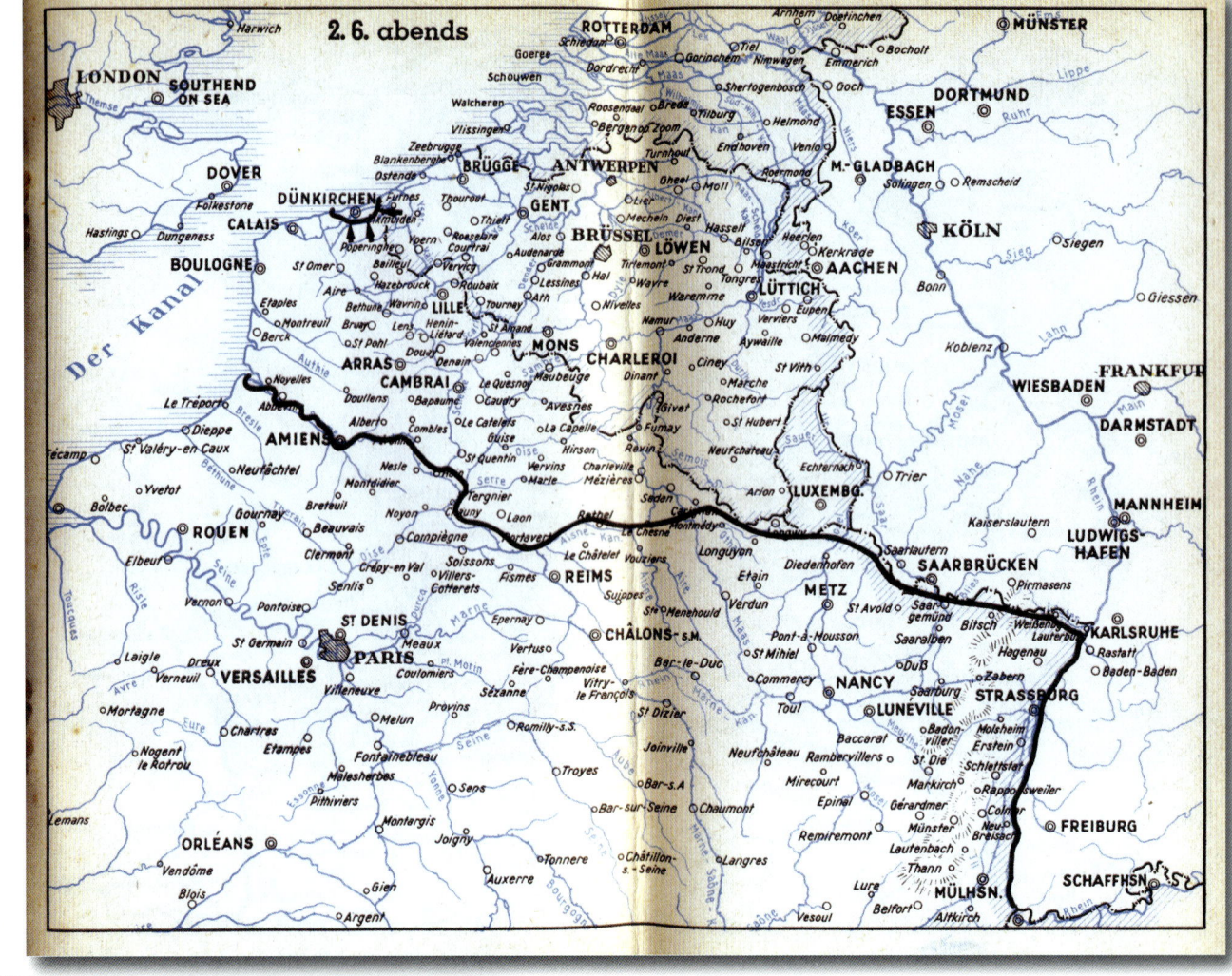

It is sometimes thought that there was no tank fighting in the area around Dunkirk before the evacuation. Here is proof to the contrary, with a knocked-out Pz 38(t) Ausf A seen close to a French Somua. The Pz 38(t) seems at first to still bear its original three-tone Czech camouflage but this is an illusion caused by the dust: it is grey and brown.

These French Somuas were abandoned by their crews near Dunkirk after a fighting retreat to the evacuation. The Germans usually collected such usable machines quite quickly, but this pair were photographed there on 20 February 1941, 8 months later.

GUDERIAN UNLEASHED

An uparmoured Pz II Ausf A or B in France. Apart from its hollow white cross, the only visible marking is a small 8 on the driver's front plate, though the pattern of its grey and brown camouflage can be seen in a few places through the dirt. It shows evidence of hard use, with quite a few scratches to its paint as well as damage to its trackguard.

A Pz III Ausf F of 1. PzDiv, whose emblem is on its turret front. It carries the white tactical number 233 with a dot but has no crosses.

PANZERWAFFE

A PzJag I of 521 PzJagAbt in France. The battalion emblem is on its side but its only other visible marking is the yellow 32 on the box mounted on its trackguard.

A full company of Pz IIs and Pz Is advance in France, with an SdKfz 251 following. They probably belong to 1 PzDiv. This is a textbook example of advancing in open order, with the platoons well separated and the tanks themselves far apart as well so that no attack can hit more than one. When or if the front platoon meets opposition, the following ones are well-placed to support them or to fan out and attack the flanks of the enemy position.

These Pz I Ausf B are seen halted on a French road, waiting for the next order.

those vehicles in contact with the Stuka formations. The fluency with which the Junkers Ju 87s of StG 77 and StG 2 were able to respond so quickly to calls for air support from the Panzers was later assessed by Richthofen's Chief of Staff to be so effective that 'never again was such a smoothly functioning system for discussing and planning joint operations achieved'. Response time to a request for air support was between 10 and 20 minutes. Arriving over the target, the dive bombers would peel off and come plummeting down on the designated targets – the banshee-like wail of their onboard 'Jericho' sirens imparting as much psychological damage to the French below as their bombs did physical harm. There can be no doubting that the success of German armour at this period was due to the marriage of these assets.

Early on the 18th, Guderian and the forces constituting his 'reconnaissance in force' – that is, 2. *Panzer Division* – had already reached St.Quentin, thereby having achieved the objective for that day set down by von Rundstedt! Unbeknown to Guderian, there was a major '*Führer* crisis' unfolding – with Halder noting in his diary that he 'is full of incomprehensible fear about the southern flank. He rages and shouts we are doing our best to ruin the entire operation and are running the risk of defeat'. In consequence, whatever permission was granted to Halder to permit Guderian to resume his westward drive – still within the remit of the 'recce in force' – severely constrained his momentum. Only late on the 19th did Hitler grudgingly grant Halder permission to 'release' the reins on Guderian, with the result that by midday on the 20th the Panzers secured Amiens unopposed. Seven hours later they rolled into Abbeville, and by midnight a battalion of 2. *Panzer* had reached the coast at Noyelles. Over a million Allied soldiers and all of their equipment were now cut off in Belgium.

Clearly, the most potent enemy with which Guderian had had to contend since the 14th had been the *Führer*'s irrational fears. In consequence the coast was reached a few days later than it would have been otherwise. Yet the arrival of German forces at the Channel had seen Hitler, according to Jodl, 'beside himself with joy'. It was as if the past few days had never happened. Now the Army and its leadership were the recipients of Hitler's fulsome praise.

However, the troubles at headquarters were not yet over. Throughout the 20th, Guderian's forces were halted once again, as this time deliberations turned on what to do next. German pressure on the Allied forces in Belgium was now coming from all points of the compass and they were being pushed towards the coast. Speculation grew that they might seek to mount attacks with armoured formations, so as to facilitate a breakout from the pocket. On the following day, Rommel's 7. *Panzer Division* was in receipt of such an attack at Arras. The reaction to it served to end the deliberations and determined German decisions for the near future.

This photograph shows a BefehlsPanzer III Ausf E, the command version of the tank with extra radios, a frame aerial and dummy main gun, and was taken at Abbeville in 1940. The unit sign on the driver's front plate is not that of 13 PzDiv, which did not serve in France and did not even exist during the French campaign, but of 13. Infantry Division, which was converted into 13. PzDiv in October 1940. The tank must have been used by 13. Artillerie Regiment, the division's organic artillery unit, as an armoured command post or front line fire control tank.

This A13 Cruiser Mark III was captured by the Germans. It displays the white rhinoceros marking of 1st Armoured Division and the unit serial 9 of 3rd Royal Tank Regiment. The '14' just visible on a yellow disc is its bridging class sign.

ROMMEL AND THE 7. PANZER DIVISION

Even as the eyes of OKW and the *Fuhrerhauptquartier* were drawn to Guderian's thrust across western France, Reinhardt's XLI. *Panzerkorps* and Hoth's XV. *Panzerkorps* had also been making tracks with their four tank divisions in the same direction, but to the north. Both formations had made problematic crossings of the

This Pz IV Ausf B or C (they cannot be told apart at this angle) is seen in a French town in May or June 1940. It carries its tactical number 414 on the old rhomboid plates as well as having them painted on its turret.

This Pz IV Ausf B of an unknown unit was knocked out near Westreham, only 18 kilometres north-east of the famous battlefield of Agincourt. The only markings on its grey and brown camouflage are the hollow white crosses.

Meuse between 12 and 14 May but, once their bridges were in place and the Panzers across in numbers, the same tale of rapid advance and disintegrating French units unfolded on their respective axes of advance as had occurred further south. Focusing on 7. *Panzer Division* will permit a closer examination of two tank versus tank encounters, one at Flavion on 15 May and one at Arras on the 21st.

Erwin Rommel had been given command of 7. *Panzer Division* in February 1940 following his posting as *Kommandant* of Hitler's headquarters. Prior to taking up his new command he had no experience of tank operations, yet Hitler had insisted, in the face of the refusal of the army personnel chief, that Rommel be given command of a Panzer Division. While no doubt many looked askance at this breach in army protocol, ascribing Rommel's appointment purely to nepotism, he was to demonstrate in the western campaign a remarkable grasp in the handling of armoured forces. From the manner in which he led from the front and manoeuvred his formations, it would seem that Rommel transferred on to his new command the insight and methods of infiltration warfare which he had practised in the Great War and written about post-war. Nor can his hell-for-leather charge across France be understood without recognising that he had a highly developed sense for self-publicity and that he intended his name to be on everyone's lips in Germany by the end of the campaign. In that he certainly succeeded.

By the morning of the 14th, Rommel's Panzers were starting their push westward from the Meuse. Having dealt with opposition during the course of their advance that day, a forward reconnaissance screen had reported back the presence of large contingents of French armour deployed astride the path of the advancing 7. *Panzer*. The French unit in question was the 1st DCR, one of the four armoured divisions that had been raised since October 1939. This formation had been despatched northward by rail on the opening day of the German offensive for the purpose of reinforcing the armour scheduled to defend the Gembloux Gap in Belgium. In the following days, and amid great confusion, the tanks of 1st DCR had been offloaded many kilometres to the south of their intended destination. It was deemed fortuitous when news came of the advance of Hoth's *Panzerkorps* from its bridgehead around Dinant that, albeit by default, it was in the right place to block the westward advance of the two Panzer Divisions. To do so it had been ordered to road-march its chargers to take position astride the German line of advance at Ermeton and Flavion. Much was expected of the DCRs. They were well-equipped, with large numbers of France's premier tank – the Char B1. But the dismal combat records of these formations in the campaign of 1940 punctured the illusion that to fight a mobile war all one needed to do was to place one's armour in tank divisions.

It took the DCR fourteen hours in low gear to reach the appointed deployment position along roads clogged with refugees fleeing westwards. By the time they did so, at 0300 hrs on the 15th, the tanks were in desperate need of refuelling. The Achilles heel of the Char B1 was its very limited range, just 96 kilometres on full tanks. Those of the 1st DCR and their attendant H39s were in the process of taking on fuel when they were hit by the tanks of 66. *PanzerAbteilung* whilst at the halt. The German tank crews later expressed their amazement that the French had done nothing to camouflage the deployment of their armour, which was used in a casual and very open fashion across a number of fields. Not only were they highly vulnerable to air strikes, which followed, but offered prime targets for the *Panzer* IIs and 38(t)s and 75mm armed *Panzer* IVs.

Under its commander, *Oberst Leutnant* Sieckenius, the 66. *PanzerAbteilung*, supported by 37mm anti-tank guns and field artillery, hit the French tanks when at their most vulnerable. With the Paks, *Panzer* IIs and *Panzer* IVs delegated to hit the refuelling wagons and personnel, the Czech-originated Pz 38(t)s employed their 37mm cannons to hit the weak spots on the French tanks as they closed to within just 200 metres of the enemy. In the case of the Char B1, the same problem of armour thickness experienced at Stonne earlier in the day by 10. *Panzer* was now encountered by 7. *Panzer*. In the same fashion, it was discovered that these French heavyweights could be disabled by a shot to the tracks or to the same weak spot of the radiator shutter on the tank's side. Every weakness of French armour described elsewhere in this text impacted on the French tank crews to an unusual extent. Slow speed, poor turret design, the lack of radios and so on, all served to undo them. The French simply had no means to match the speed and manoeuvrability of the Panzers moving as a body and operating as a combined-arms formation. The French difficulties were compounded by the arrival of 5. *Panzer Division*, although they had recovered enough for some of their number to give this Panzer formation a bit of a bloody nose before they succumbed.

Rommel, however, did not stay to observe the fighting. He merely by passed Flavion and, once 5. *Panzer* had arrived on the scene, pulled out Sieckenius and ordered him to rejoin the main thrust of 7. *Panzer*. Later in the day, other tanks from the same DCR inflicted heavier losses on the Germans in an encounter at Ermeton further to the west. Even that did not slow down Rommel. Plunging on, in the van of the advance in his command *Panzer* III or SPW, he constantly demanded speed, speed!' '*Angriff, angriff!*' – 'Attack, attack' – a refrain that his tank commanders would recall with a degree of wry amusement in the Western Desert! Always *Angriff*! On an approach to a village, or passing woods that flanked the road or through which his tanks had to drive, he ordered his crews to fire their weapons for all they were worth. It seems that the psychological impact of this blizzard of random fire had its impact on the French defending such places. In most cases, they simply upped and ran. According to Rommel, it spared the lives of his men. One observer later wrote an account that provides insight into Rommel's *modus operandi*:

These close-ups of Char 2C number 99 show the unusual method of rail transport adopted for these large tanks. Instead of carrying them on wagons, removable mounts were attached to their fronts and rears as adapters for special railway bogies.

Below: This view of number 99 shows the complicated form of the Char 2C's engine deck.

At least one Char 2C was used for tests of French armour plate's resistance to German anti-tank guns. The results were felt to be positive but were rather misleading, since the Char 2Cs were not armoured up to 1940 standards.

A close-up view of the Char used in the anti-tank test (opposite page bottom). It is minus its tracks and a portion of its lower skirts.

A Kfz 13 armoured car brings up the rear of a column of SdKfz 222 armoured cars in France. It is camouflaged in grey and brown, seen most clearly on the cover of its spare wheel, and shows the tactical sign for an armoured car unit on one rear mudguard and the G insignia of a unit of General Guderian's army group on the other.

Here are a Pz II Ausf A or B and a Pz 35 (t) of 6. PzDiv advancing in France. Their crews are wary of friendly fire from the Luftwaffe and have displayed Nazi flags on the engine decks instead of the normal white air recognition rectangle. The Pz 35 (t)'s flag almost hides its white tactical number 322 on a rhomboid plate and the yellow division sign beside it of an inverted Y with two dots beside it.

A Pz II Ausf A or B in France. The muzzles of its guns have been wrapped in cloth to keep dust out of them, so no enemy is expected nearby. The white turret number of 1103 indicates a headquarters tank of the second battalion of its regiment, and the underlining may denote the second regiment of its Division.

The French Renault UE supply carrier was built in large numbers and many were captured. Many of them were used by the Germans for carrying supplies and as light gun tractors, at least as late as 1942, and some were converted with new added superstructures as observation posts and machine gun carriers for airfield defence – in which role they were still serving when found on the Normandy airfields after D-Day.

'I have never seen anything like the scenes along Rommel's route of advance. His tanks had run into a French division coming down the same road, and they had just kept advancing on right past it. For the next eight or nine kilometres there were hundreds of trucks and tanks some driven into ditches, others burnt out, many still carrying dead and injured. More and more Frenchmen came out of the fields with abject fear written on their faces and their hands in the air. From up front came the short sharp crack of the guns of our tanks, which Rommel was personally directing – standing upright in his ACV with two staff officers, his cap pushed back, urging everybody ahead'.

In the same manner that Guderian's tactics upset the *Feldherren* in the OKH, so too did Rommel's and Reinhardt's. These Panzer generals seemed to be a law unto themselves. It was not acceptable! There was a chain of command and it had to be respected! Under *Fall Rot,* the OKH would move to ensure that these characters would toe the line!

On 18 May, the leading element of Rommel's forces had halted within sight of the town of Le Cateau, a name which carried great resonance for the British going back to 1914. Two days later he came up against them for the first time. On the 21st, he was at Arras when they launched an armoured counter-attack against his force. It was to become a memorable encounter.

THE ALLIED COUNTER-STROKE AT ARRAS

In his book '*Blitzkrieg Legend*', Karl Heinz Frieser prefaces his account of the battle of Arras with the sub-heading: 'A tactical failure with unsuspected operational consequences'. This concise assessment of the clash succinctly catches the significance of the encounter. In no way militarily decisive, when set against the backdrop of fear and expectation of just such an Allied response ever since 14 May, it is not surprising that its impact on the German higher command was to provoke them to resolve the discussion over the direction of future operations.

By 20 May the pressure of the German forces in Belgium was rapidly propelling the Allied forces back towards the Channel coast. Recognising the warning signs, the British had informed the French the day before that they intended to withdraw as much of their Expeditionary Force as they could in the days ahead. This affected French morale in a profound way. What clearer indication could they have that their closest ally believed the battle to be lost. Indeed, the pressure on the encircled Allied forces was mounting by the day.

In Belgium Hoeppner's *Panzerkorps* was finally able to push through the Gembloux Gap, following in the wake of the French forces now pulling back to the north. Now subordinated to Army Group A, it followed in the wake of Hoth's two Panzer Divisions, which were in turn being led by Rommel's 7. *Panzer*. Although Gamelin was replaced that day by General Maxime Weygand, the counter-attack at Arras was only part of a wider counter offensive that he had planned before his departure. Given the circumstances, it was by way of an improvised affair with British and French pulling together what they had to hand in the way of armour. For the former, Arras was of great importance as it was the main base of the B.E.F in Belgium and was stocked with supplies needed as it pulled back to the coast pending its evacuation. An attempt by Rommel to take the town by a coup de main on the 20th was stopped by the British defenders, in consequence of which he diverted his Panzers to the south so as to bypass the town.

When finally launched, Allied armour ploughed straight into the unprotected flank of the German infantry following behind the Panzers. Unsurprisingly, its impact was profound. The British element of the attacking force comprised 88 Infantry Tank Mark Is – a small, slow, machine gun-armed, 11 ton, infantry support vehicle – nicknamed 'Matilda', and a small number of the more formidable Matilda Mk IIs. Weighing in at 26 tons, the latter's extremely heavy armour (for the time) of 20mm through to 78mm on the hull front made them absolutely impervious to any German guns except the 88mm Flak or heavy artillery pieces firing over open sights. French armour was provided in the form of Somuas and H35s – the last survivors of Prioux's 3rd DLM which had held up Hoeppner's Panzer Divisions at Hannut, just six days before.

In the absence of his infantry, which should have arrived at his forward position, Rommel returned to his rear to find it already under attack by the Anglo-French force. In reality, the German lines were assailed by a three column armoured assault. Unbeknown to the Germans, the Allied force did not know much about the force it was attacking, having had no time to undertake any pre–attack reconnaissance. Furthermore the lack of radios in the French tanks prevented them from co-ordinating their efforts, and the tiredness of the supporting infantry tended to see them left behind as the tanks moved forward.

As soon as the Allied attack began, it got into trouble. Confusion led to 7RTR (7th Royal Tank Regiment) getting lost on the way to its start line, in consequence of which the formation lost its coherence. When finally it approached the German positions, it was quite disorganised and the tanks were unable to support each other. The third and outmost column, made up of the Somuas and H35s of 3rd DLM, hung back, then moved in behind the moving chaos of 7RTR and joined their assault on the German 7th Rifle Regiment. It was the German positions established directly to the south of Arras that the Matilda IIs of 4RTR struck. A screen of 37mm Pak 36 anti-tank guns protected the German forces positioned here and, despite the efforts of their crews, the Pak gunners watched helplessly as their shells just bounced off the frontal armour of the Matildas. For the first time in the campaign, tank fright and panic was now visited on the Germans. The Matildas drove through and over the German defenders. Anti-tank guns were crushed, their crews and supporting infantry killed by machine gun fire, and 2-pounder main guns shot up and set fire to vehicles and lorries. In all, the Germans were being hit by an arc of enemy armour that threatened to break through 7. *Panzer*'s line.

Rommel now showed his mettle as a commander and his actions proved the wisdom of leading from the front. Not only did his presence encourage his men but also his orders were carried out, virtually on the spot. Frieser, in his account of the battle, identifies four things that Rommel did which helped turn the battle in his favour.

His first decision was to order the construction of a containment line of anti-tank guns and light Flak weapons. He radioed his divisional headquarters and ordered then to set up a second containment line composed of 88mm Flak weapons and 105mm and 150mm artillery pieces.

At 1600, he had called for air support in the form of Stuka strikes on the enemy tank formations. However, given their commitments elsewhere they only arrived two hours later. By then, mainly the 88s in the second containment line had broken the back of the Allied attack. Nonetheless, the Stukas pounced on the surviving armour as it pulled back to its start lines. Frieser noted that the Stukas had carried out no less than 300 sorties by 2030 hrs.

Rommel recalled 25. *Panzer Regiment* and ordered its commander, *Oberst* Karl Rothenburg, to cut off the retreat of the Allied armour. By the time, this formation had turned back and moved against the enemy right flank 25. PzRgt found itself in combat with the remnants of the 3rd DLM's armour which comprised of about 60 Somuas and H35s. On this occasion, it came off second best, suffering heavy losses. By then darkness was falling and the battle of Arras petered out in the gathering gloom.

In dealing with the Matildas Rommel had learnt a trick about employment of the 88mm Flak which he would later use to devastating effect in the western desert. After Arras, this weapon would be employed ever more frequently as a 'tank killer'. It also became the chosen calibre of weapon on all future heavy tanks, heavy tank destroyers and tank hunters. Just twenty-eight British tanks returned to their start lines – thus registering a loss of sixty Matildas during the course of the battle. The Germans had weathered the Allied attack, but the losses to 7. *Panzer Division* were the greatest they experienced in the campaign.

In consequence of the attack on Arras, all further debate about the near future direction of the German attack was resolved with the decision to order Guderian's Panzer Divisions to move north-east and capture the Channel ports. However, this would be carried out without 10. *Panzer Division*, which was pulled back to provide a Panzer group reserve in the event that Arras had not been a 'one-off'. This effectively stymied the plan which Guderian had already formulated, in that he had earmarked this formation to rapidly advance on, and capture, Dunkirk. 1. *Panzer* was to advance on Calais and 2. *Panzer* was to move against Boulogne. By the 21st, German intelligence had ascertained that the B.E.F. would be evacuated through the port of Dunkirk. 10. *Panzer's* absence from Guderian's short-term order of battle was thus to impact mightily on the events of the next fortnight.

Hesitation and indecision in the wake of the Arras attack now affected the nerve of OKH and von Rundstedt. It was only on the 22nd that Guderian was given the green light to move against the two nearest Channel ports. 2. *Panzer* moved against Boulogne in the afternoon of that day, but was unable to secure the port in the face of very strong resistance from Allied troops who knew by now that every hour they delayed the enemy would aid their comrades withdrawing on Dunkirk. Boulogne held out for another thirty-six hours. The same level of resistance was encountered in the attempt to take Calais. This port held out through to the evening of the 26th.

On 22 May, 10. *Panzer Division* was released by Kleist from its reserve role and given back to Guderian, who immediately sent it to Calais to relieve 1. *Panzer*. This division was then ordered, in its turn, to move on Dunkirk via Gravelines. By the 24th Guderian's Panzers had advanced so that they were just 24 kilometres from the port, with every expectation that it would fall to them the following day. Then, inexplicably, the Panzers were ordered to halt once again. It is not the place here to enter into a discussion of the whys and wherefores of this decision, most notably the halt orders issued to the Panzers. Suffice to say that it was only on the 27th, after three wasted days (from the German perspective) that the Panzers were permitted once more to resume their advance, with Dunkirk the given objective. However, in those three days the Allies had been able to improve the defences of the port sufficiently to deny the Germans their prize until 4 June. By then, 330,000 Allied troops had been evacuated from Dunkirk's port and beaches. It was the halt order that had made this possible. Without a doubt this was the greatest error the Germans made in the Western campaign. Although the British Army had been forced to abandon all of its equipment, the manpower that had been saved would provide the nucleus of a new Army which would return to the continent just four years later.

Even before the fall of Dunkirk, OKH had turned its sights on planning for stage two of the battle for France. Codenamed *Fall Rot* (Case Red), the purpose was simple – to administer the *coup de grace* to a tottering nation whose cause was now beyond redemption.

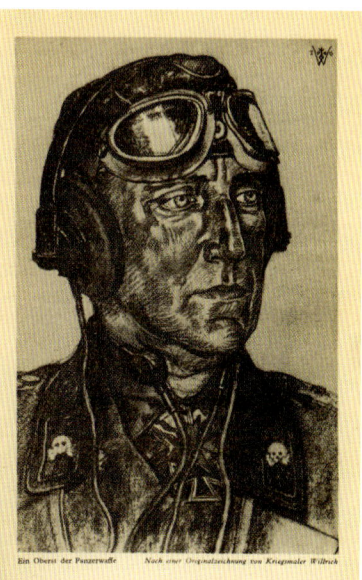

'Ein Oberst der Panzerwaffe': a contemporary image from the pages of a German book published in 1940 on the invasion of France by Dr. Kurt Hesse (see Publisher's Note at the bottom of page two).

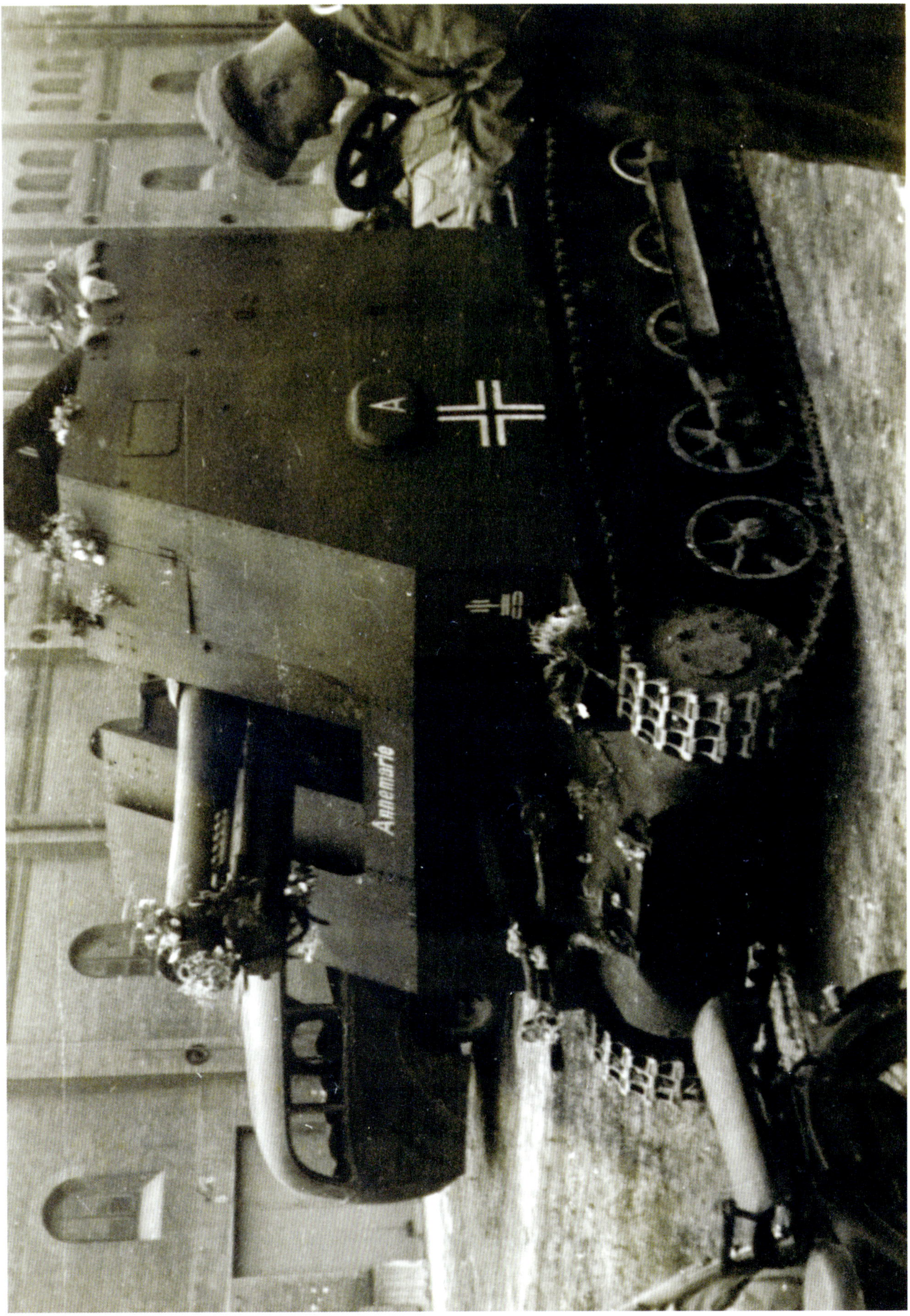
A
Annemarie

GUDERIAN UNLEASHED

sIG33 (Sf) auf PzKpfw. 1 Ausf. B

Weight: 8.5 tonnes
Crew: 4 onboard + 3 on ammunition vehicle
Engine: Maybach NL 38 TR, 100 HP
Speed: 25 km/h approx
Armament: 15 cm sIG 33
Length: 4.42 m
Width: 2.60 m
Height: 3.35 m
Armour: 10 to 13mm

The 15 cm sIG33 (Sf) auf PzKpfw. 1 Ausf. B (15 cm heavy infantry gun (self-propelled) on a Pz I Ausf B chassis) is better known as the Bison I. This one belonged to sIGKp (mot) 706 (heavy infantry gun (motorised) Company 706) of 10 PzDiv and is seen in a French town. Its grey and brown camouflage is relieved only by the white-and-black cross, the diagonal yellow bar of the division's emblem and the white K of a vehicle serving with Kampfgruppe Kleist (Army Group von Kleist). Some Bisons of this unit are known to have carried names on their front armour below the gun, but this one does not even show the usual letter denoting which gun it was in the battery.
The yellow bar and white K were repeated on the starboard side of the front armour together with the battery number 706.

© COPYRIGHT HILARY LOUIS DOYLE

Denouement – *'Fall Rot'*

This Pz IV Ausf D and Pz II Ausf A or B were photographed in the ruins of Vitry, France. They belong to PzRegt 8 of 10 PzDiv and both display on their turret rears the Roman III identifying the Regiment's 3rd company, though the wolfsangel regimental emblem beside the III is partly hidden by equipment on the Pz II and completely hidden by the unit-made stowage box of the Pz IV. No tactical number is visible on the Pz II but the Pz IV carries 313 in yellow painted directly on to its superstructure side. Although both tanks belong to the same company, their wide-armed white crosses differ, the Pz IV's being simply painted on to the grey and brown camouflage while the Pz II's is filled in with black. Standardisation, even within a unit, was still a thing of the future.

PHASE TWO of the German campaign against France – codenamed *Fall Rot* – was concerned with forcing the formal surrender of France, which had already been defeated in fact. In this second phase, although the *Panzerwaffe* played its part, it did not assume the central role that it had in Case Yellow.

Of the Allied forces which had moved into Belgium less than a month before, sixty-one divisions had been destroyed. To the prisoner total of 1,200,000 men was added equipment amounting to three-quarters of the best tanks and artillery the Allies possessed. Consequently what is beyond doubt is that the French Army no longer possessed the resources to withstand the *Wehrmacht* when *Rot* was launched on 5 June. Seventeen days later, it was all over.

The German redeployment of their forces for the second phase was rapid. In its final form, the plan saw all three army groups committed to the offensive, albeit with staggered start dates. A total of 142 divisions would be launched against a French total of just 64. The latter were so stretched in defending a front of 965 kilometres that Weygand had no reserves to spare to address a German breakthrough, wherever and whenever it took place. Despite the overwhelming success of the *Panzerkorps* in Phase One, no provision was made in *Fall Rot* for them to operate in independent formations. Other than a transfer of divisional assets, the mobile formations were firmly shackled, with oversight of their operations granted to Army control. There were no major tank battles in this second phase.

The offensive began with Army Group B attacking on either side of Paris and driving for the Seine. Among its 47 divisions it now possessed the greatest number of mobile formations. *Panzergruppe* Kleist was fielding two corps, each with two Panzer Divisions. XV. *Panzerkorps*, under Hoth, retained the 5. and 7. *Panzer Divisions*. It was the latter formation that was first to reach the river Seine on 10 June, with 7. *Panzer* in the van. Rommel's progress had been rapid, his division employing their commander's patent '*Flächenmarsch*' – in which the whole Division moved forward en masse, in a box formation. Such was its rapidity that on some days it advanced up to 80 kilometres. However, a feature of the second phase was the manner in which almost all German infantry formations moved forward, at a remarkable pace, in many cases following on the heels of the advancing mobile formations extremely quickly with some divisions marching up to 48 kilometres per day.

This is a Pz III Befehlspanzer Ausf E of PzRegt 8 in 10 PzDiv, seen near Tours in France. This version of the tank replaced the main gun and all three machine guns with a dummy main gun and one dummy machine gun in the turret, beside a single machine gun in a ball mount, and a pistol port in the hull front. This made room for a map board and more powerful radio equipment inside the tank.

This is a Pz III Ausf F of 1 PzDiv in Montmeilland, France, on 9 June 1940. It displays all its markings in white: hollow wide-armed cross, turret number 544 and division emblem. The divisions between its grey and brown colours can be faintly seen.

But the semblance of overwhelming superiority was in some aspects more apparent than real, being disguised only by the weakness of the enemy. There was once again hesitation, indecision and misdirection but above all the oversight and interference in OKH's affairs by Hitler. Guderian was again frustrated by the evidence of the continuing perception of the *Panzerwaffe* still as an adjunct of the infantry. Although his forces had begun their assault on 9 June as scheduled it was not until a day later, due to problems caused by crossing the river Aisne, that his *Panzergruppe* began its advance.

As early as the 12th, Weygand had already stated that an armistice should be sought, to prevent the chaos now impacting on the civilian population spreading to the Army. Paris was declared an open city, and on 14 June it fell to the Germans. On the same day, von Bock ordered his mobile forces to advance into Brittany and Normandy. This saw 7. *Panzer* – by now nicknamed 'the Ghost division' because of the rapidity of its advance and the manner in which for the enemy 'it just seemed to pop up' anywhere – directed towards Normandy. A few days after, Rommel forced the surrender of a large number of British and French troops at St. Valery. On 16 June, 7. *Panzer* crossed the Seine and pushed west from Rouen. Against a backdrop of rumoured French requests for an armistice, he once again pushed his division day and night. Two days later, having traversed the length of Normandy and up the Cherbourg peninsula, he captured that port.

Guderian's *Panzergruppe* had initially been delayed in crossing the river Aisne at the start of Army Group A's offensive on 9 June. Thereafter his tanks had advanced on the river Marne and, having crossed this, his forces drove southward towards the Swiss border. Here the biggest problems arose not from enemy opposition but from the traffic confusion generated by tank and infantry units becoming caught up with each other. It would seem that neither OKH nor the respective Army commands which oversaw Panzer operations had yet learnt to give tanks priority in route planning. The Panzers were, however, instrumental in helping to bring about the biggest encirclement of French forces in *Fall Rot* when, with the assistance of Army Group C, Army A pinned half a million French soldiers against the Maginot Line before they surrendered on 22 June. On the same day, the French accepted the German armistice terms.

German Panzer losses for May – June 1940

	Panzer 1	Panzer II	Panzer III	Panzer IV	Pz.35(t)	Pz.38(t)	Totals
May/June	182	250	135	97	62	69	795 written-off

86 PANZERWAFFE

A contemporary map (of a series) published in a German book in 1940 – 'Forward over the Battlefield' on the invasion of France. The map shows the German front line on the evening of 22 June – the date the French surrendered. See Publisher's Note at the bottom of page two.

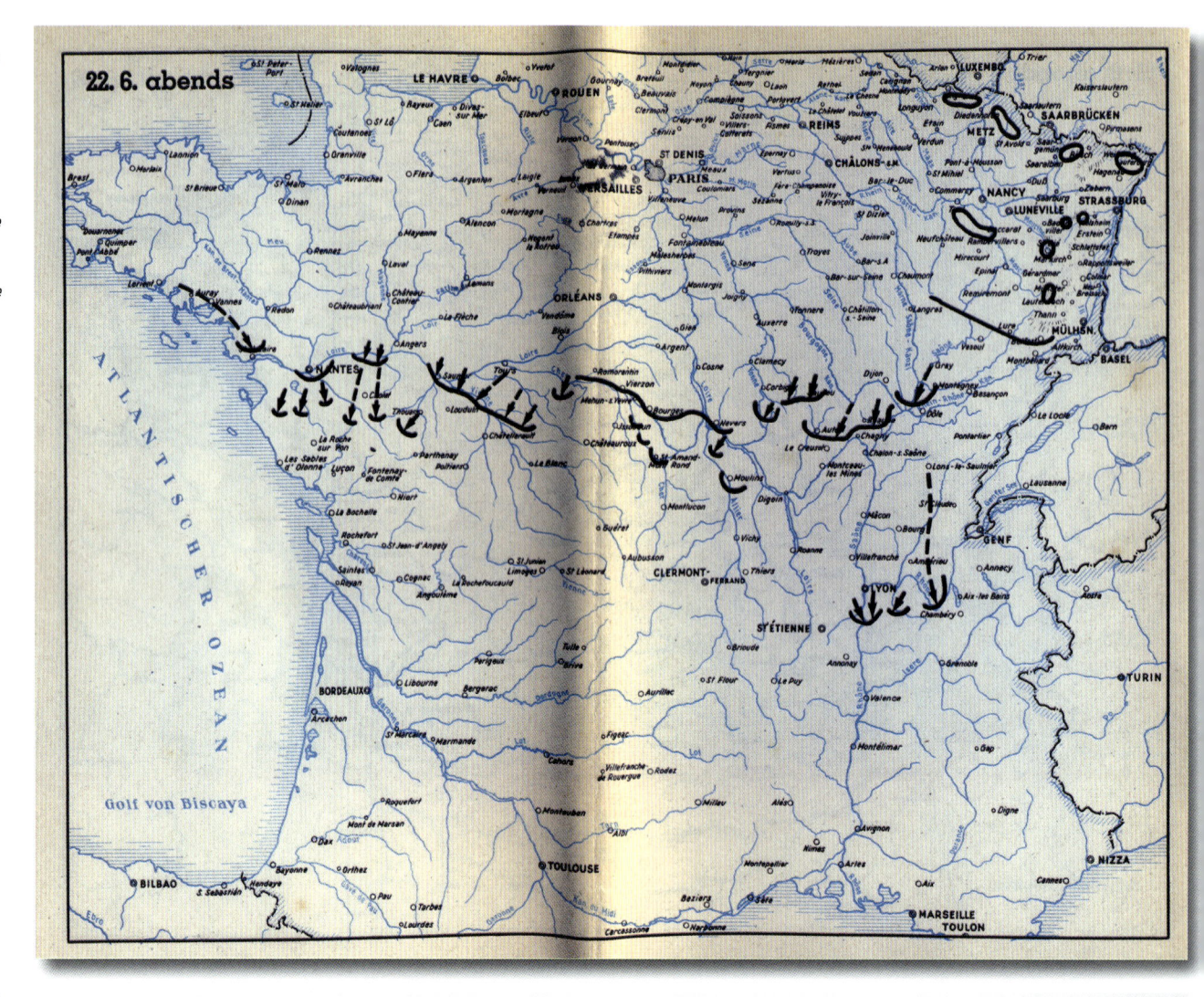

This Befehlspanzer III Ausf E, photographed in a French vineyard, gives a good view of the ball-mounted machine gun that replaced its normal turret armament. The use of dummy guns gave much more space inside for the radios and map table needed by unit commanders. The frame aerial for its radios can just be seen behind its turret but a canvas sheet hides the entire superstructure front.

A Pz IV Ausf C moving through a wrecked French town and followed by a Pz II Ausf A or B. The Pz IV has the small white tactical number 431 on its side in front of its hollow white cross.

This French Char B1 was blown up by its crew after running out of fuel, allowing a view into its engine compartment.

PANZERWAFFE

DENOUEMENT-FALL ROT

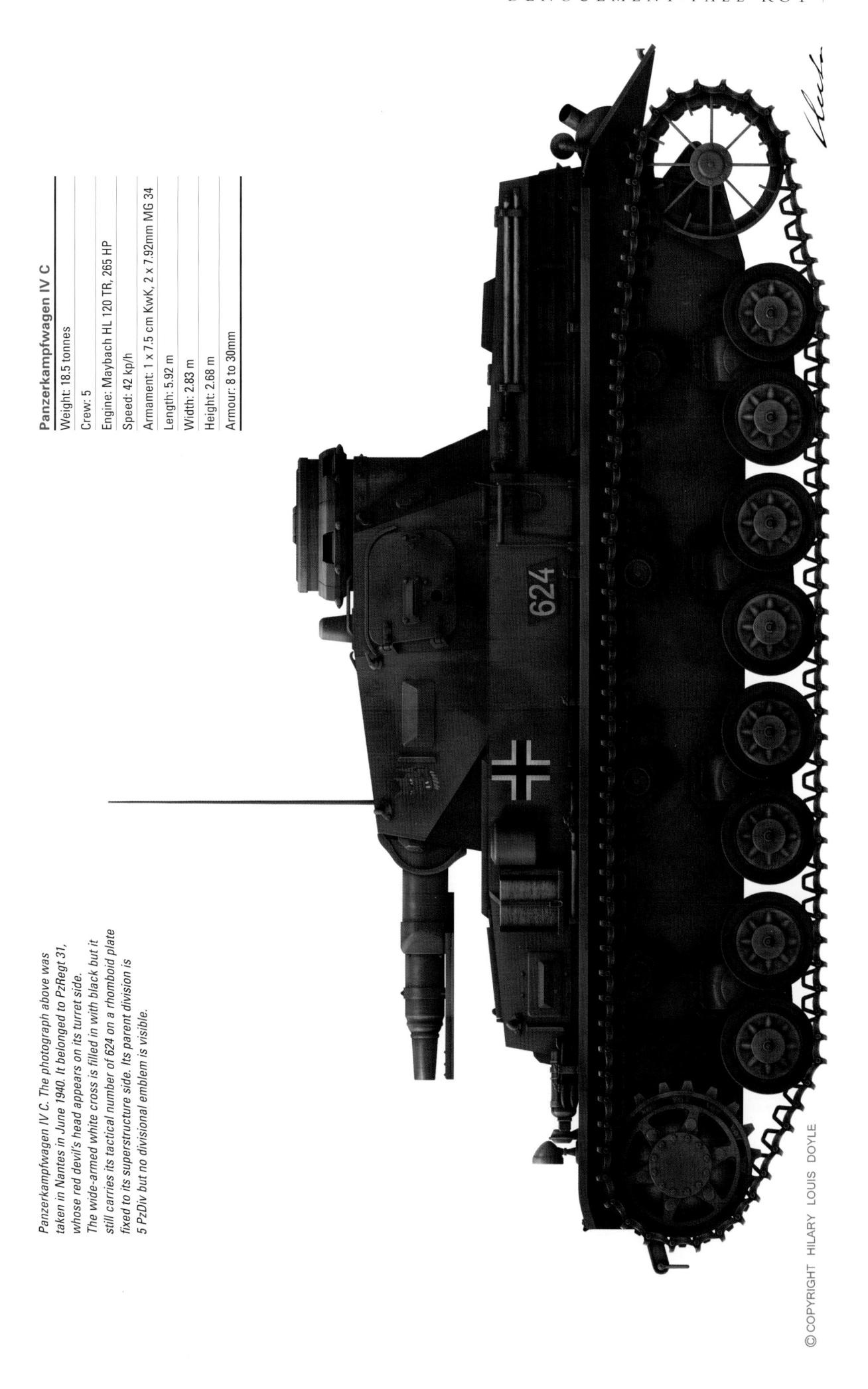

Panzerkampfwagen IV C
Weight: 18.5 tonnes
Crew: 5
Engine: Maybach HL 120 TR, 265 HP
Speed: 42 kp/h
Armament: 1 x 7.5 cm KwK, 2 x 7.92mm MG 34
Length: 5.92 m
Width: 2.83 m
Height: 2.68 m
Armour: 8 to 30mm

Panzerkampfwagen IV C. The photograph above was taken in Nantes in June 1940. It belonged to PzRegt 31, whose red devil's head appears on its turret side. The wide-armed white cross is filled in with black but it still carries its tactical number of 624 on a rhomboid plate fixed to its superstructure side. Its parent division is 5 PzDiv but no divisional emblem is visible.

© COPYRIGHT HILARY LOUIS DOYLE

PANZERWAFFE

French anti-tank guns had proved too effective for some Panzer crews' peace of mind, so the men of this Pz IV Ausf C have added sandbags and spare track links to the front of their tank. Its grey and brown camouflage can be seen on the turret front.

A Pz IV Ausf A moving through a French town.

DENOUEMENT–FALL ROT

The driver of this Pz II Ausf A or B demonstrates that it was quite possible for him to escape through the hatch on its glacis.

This Pz IV Ausf D was photographed on 20 June 1940 near Neuvelles, south-east of Paris.

This Pz I Ausf B of 3 PzDiv is seen on its victorious return to its home base in Germany on 10 July 1940. The significance of the date in white, 5.6.40, beside its yellow division sign is unknown.

Panzers for Seelöwe

WITHIN a month of the French surrender Hitler issued his Directive No: 16 'on preparations for a landing operation against England'. The Army's role was to 'draw up the operational and crossing plans for all formations of the first wave of the invasion'.

Included in that first wave were to be a formation of 248 Panzers. These *Tauchpanzers* – submersible tanks – consisted of *Panzer* IIs, and medium *Panzer* IIIs and IVs. In the case of the light Panzers, they were fitted with specially designed floats which enabled them to be dropped off from an invasion barge from which they would proceed to the shore.

The medium tanks however, being heavier, were equipped with a more complex system which enabled them to be dropped off shore from a freight barge where the maximum depth of the sea was 15 metres or less. Steps to seal the tanks involved the following: all openings such as visors were made watertight with rubber seals and cable tar; the turret hatches were secured from within by inside bolts which had to be released once ashore; a special rubber coating was applied to the commander's cupola, the gun mantlet and the machine gun position; and an inflated rubber tube sealed the joint between the turret base and the hull. Once ashore these fittings could be removed extremely quickly by use of explosive fuses. The crew were all equipped with life-saving equipment of the type issued to U-Boat crewmembers.

Fresh air was drawn into the tank when underwater via a 200-metre long rubber hose that snaked to the surface and was there attached to a buoy, which also had a radio antenna. This was to help aid direction of the tank when underwater, with a controller on the surface passing on instructions through the radio link. Water was prevented from entering the exhaust pipes by the fitment of special one-way pressure valves. The engine itself was kept cool when underwater by the use of a sea water system which was switched on from within the tank, with any excess water being drained off via a sump pump.

Four submersible tank battalions were created on 15 July 1940, with each being allocated a letter-code A through D. However, the first of these was only formed at Putlos in September and October with volunteers drawn from Panzer Regiment 2 of 1. *Panzer Division*. The others followed shortly thereafter. The postponement of *Seelöwe* saw these vehicles become temporarily redundant. They were re-incorporated into the *Panzerwaffe* with the units renamed and subsumed under Panzer Brigade 1 of 1. *Panzer Division*. They would, however, see use in June 1941 in the invasion of Russia when a number of the *Panzer* IIIs and IVs were employed to cross the river Bug.

THE REORGANISATION OF THE PANZERWAFFE

The most radical and far-reaching change to the *Panzerwaffe* came when by a stroke of his pen, Hitler, already thinking in terms of a Russian campaign the following year, signed a document doubling the number of Panzer Divisions. This decision was made official by the OKH on 26 September 1940. This was not, however, to be brought about by a massive expansion of tank production – we have already seen how in the short term that was not possible. Rather, it was to be realised in part by the simple expedient of taking away the second Panzer regiment of those six Panzer Divisions that had two Panzer regiments. These would provide the core of six new divisions. The four other Panzer Divisions kept their Panzer regiments. New regiments were created for four other Panzer Divisions. The newly created divisions and the origin of their core formations are given below.

- **11. PzDiv:** established on 1 Aug 1940. Core of the new formation came from 15th PzRgt/5th Pz.Div.
- **12. PzDiv:** established in Oct 1940. Core of new formation came from the 2nd Mot. Inf.Div.
- **13. PzDiv:** established in Vienna on 11 Oct 1940. Core of new formation came from 4th PzRgt/2nd PzDiv and parts of 13th Mot. Inf.Div.
- **14. PzDiv**: established in August 1940. Core of new formation came from 36th PzRgt /4th PzDiv and 4th Inf.Div.
- **15. PzDiv:** established by March 1941. Core of new formation came from 8th Pz.Rgt/3rd PzDiv and 33rd Inf.Div.
- **16. PzDiv:** authorised in August 1940. Core of new formation provided by 2nd batt.2nd PzRgt/Ist PzDiv and 16th Inf.Div.
- **17. PzDiv:** established in Nov 1940. Core of formation came from replacement battalions of the 4th and 33 rd PzRgts and 27th Inf.Div.
- **18. PzDiv:** formed on 26 Oct 1940. Core of formation used the four battalions of *Tauchpanzers*.
- **19. PzDiv:** Formed in Nov 1940 in Hannover. Core provided by 19th Inf. Div. Panzer element came from 10th, 11th, and 25th *Ersatz* (replacement) *Pz.Abteilungen*.
- **20. PzDiv:** Formed from parts of 19th Inf.Div–not used in formation of 19th PzDiv. Core of PzRgt. came from three abt. of 21st PzRgt, which had in their turn come from 7th and 35th *Ersatz PzAbteilungen*.

In addition, to partner these new divisions, the 3rd, 10th, 14th, 18th, 25th and 36th Infantry Divisions were translated into Motorised Infantry Divisions (later designated Panzer Grenadier Divisions). This process of reorganisation, took some while to complete, with the 10th, 18th and 36th Motorised Infantry Divisions not being fully organised and trained until the late spring of 1941. Not surprisingly, given the low level of

This Pz IV Ausf D seen in France was probably photographed well after the invasion, since it carries the turret-rear stowage bin not officially provided for the troops to fit until 1941. However, it still bears its invasion-period rhomboid plate for the white tactical number 902, though the plate has been trimmed, and the white hollow cross often used at that time.

A Pz I Ausf A converted to a Munitionspanzer by the replacement of its turret with a double hatch is seen with a group of Gebirgsjäger mountain troops near Wimereaux in France. Munitionspanzers were supposed to be used for carrying ammunition, but these men seem to be keen on taking a ride!

production of armour and wheeled vehicles, these formations and 18. and 20. *Panzer Divisions* received their allotted equipment in phases – a matter that did not aid effective training.

Although doubling the size of the tank arm, this reorganisation did not profoundly impact on the size of the tank park. Numbers of Panzers did not show a significant increase beyond the total available at the start of *Fall Gelb*. However, by June 1941 and the launch of *Barbarossa*, there were far fewer of the light Panzers in combat formations and more of the medium tanks. It did, however, lead to a generally uniform organisation of the Panzer Divisions – with most now having one Panzer regiment of two battalions – although there were exceptions to the rule with both 6. *Panzer*'s and 20. Panzer's tank regiments fielding three battalions.

For Guderian this was very much a backward step. Although superficially increasing the strength of the *Panzerwaffe* 'overnight', in his view it served to detract from their effectiveness. There were two primary reasons why, in his opinion, the two-regiment Panzer Division was both more effective and thus more efficient. In respect of the former, experience in France had shown that even when a Panzer Division suffered substantial losses – as had Hoeppner's two divisions between 12 and 15 May in Belgium – the large number of Panzers remaining in each division still permitted them to retain a high degree of combat effectiveness. It followed that the new division, equipped with only half as many tanks, would see their effectiveness degrade far more rapidly when faced with a similar reduction in their numbers through combat. This would be seen very shortly after the start of Barbarossa.

Furthermore, doubling the size of the *Panzerwaffe* merely served to exacerbate an already severe problem German industry had in providing an adequate supply of wheeled vehicles to service the logistic needs of each formation. Prior to *Fall Gelb* this had proved to be a massive headache at OKH, with the Army being allocated a paltry number of lorries each month to service all of its needs – let alone those of an expanded tank arm – from the total number produced by the national automotive industry. The need to provide every Panzer Division with an adequate lorry park saw more or less every serviceable captured vehicle – from passenger cars through to heavy lorries – impressed into service as substitutes for the machines that Opel, Henschel, Büssing–Nag and other German producers were unable to supply. As from 1941, this reality is attested to in photographs in which a plethora of impressed types can be seen serving with the *Panzerwaffe* wherever they were deployed. Furthermore, the provision of spares needed to service such a diverse range of vehicles proved to be a logistic nightmare and the matter only got worse, not better, as the war progressed.

Improving the panzers

In the light of combat experience from the campaign it was necessary to improve the Panzers. One of these needs was clearly in the field of armament. We have already seen that production of the 50mm L/42 cannon for the *Panzer* III Ausf G only started coming off the production line in July 1940. While this was an upgrade that provided the *Panzer* III with a weapon which was more effective than the 37mm that had been found

This Pz IV Ausf B is in a town in the Aube region of France on 15 June 1940. It carries the yellow turret number 846 and a wide-armed hollow white cross on its grey and brown camouflage. The emblem on the driver's front plate appears to be that used in France by 4 PzDiv.

'...und drüben liegt England' (and over there lies England) reads the type (lower left) of this image. It is the last to be found at the back of the German book published in 1940 on the invasion of France by Dr. Kurt Hesse (see Publisher's Note on page two). It is this book which provided the maps for this volume.

so wanting, experience across the board with the more heavily armoured French and British tanks had pointed to the need for a weapon of heavier calibre. However, one was not available at the time. Nor was the *Panzer* III, because of its small hull and turret ring, able to mount a weapon of higher calibre and velocity (although the last model of the *Panzer* III, the Ausf N, would mount a 75mm weapon, it was the same short L/24 calibre originally carried by the early models of the *Panzer* IV).

Although by late 1940, the 50mm L/60 was in production, it was not fitted to the *Panzer* III, which continued to be equipped with the 50mm L/42 after July 1940. Hitler had ordered that the L/60 be fitted into the *Panzer* III in 1940, but the *Heereswaffenamt* decided that this weapon should first be given to the infantry as an anti-tank gun. This became the 50mm Pak 38. The first *Panzer* III to be built with this weapon therefore did not leave the production lines until December 1941. This was seven months after the start of *Barbarossa*. Had the L/60 armed *Panzer* III been available in numbers in June 1941, the *Panzerwaffe* would have been far more able to cope with the appearance of the technologically more advanced T-34 and KV series that were encountered by the Germans before the end of June 1941. These provided a massive shock to the *Panzerwaffe*'s smug presumption that the *Panzer* III and IV were more than adequate to see out the war. Hitler's discovery in April 1941 that his order that the *Panzer* III be equipped with the 50mm Pak 38 had been deliberately sidestepped by the *Heereswaffenamt* generated in him a distrust of that department which lasted through to the end of the conflict.

The German tank arm had emerged from the French Campaign with its exploits lauded in Goebbels' press and its reputation profoundly enhanced. Even those who had looked askance, and had viewed Guderian and his coterie of supporters as the over-vocal champions of an upstart arm, now began to view the *Panzerwaffe* in a new light. Certainly, Hitler's faith in this instrument accounts for his decision to double its size. There was also the sense that possibly the Germans had hit upon a formula that could grant them victory. Perhaps there was, after all, something of substance to the term '*Blitzkrieg*'. In the weeks of elation following the defeat of France there were few cool heads in Germany. A more sober and objective examination of the campaign may well have prompted some serious thinking and a real effort to think beyond the façade of invincibility and hubris that now seemed to cloak the *Wehrmacht*. The British historian Adam Tooze in his book 'The Wages of Destruction' makes a number of very telling observations about the French Campaign:

'The victory of 1940 is not a mysterious event explicable only in terms of the uncanny élan of the German army and the unwillingness of the French to fight. The odds facing Germany were not good. However, they were not so bad that they could not be overcome by superior planning and manoeuvre.

A close analysis of the mechanics of the *Blitzkrieg* reveals the astonishing degree of concentration achieved, but also the enormous gamble that Hitler and the *Wehrmacht* leadership were taking on 10 May. Precisely because it involved such a concentrated use of force, Manstein's plan was a 'one-shot affair'. If the initial assault had failed, and it could have failed in many ways, the *Wehrmacht* as an offensive force would have been spent. The gamble paid off. However, contrary to appearances the Germans had not discovered a patent recipe for military miracles. The overwhelming success of May 1940, resulting in the defeat of a major European power in a matter of weeks, was not a repeatable outcome. In fact, when we appreciate the huge risks involved in Manstein's plan, the attack on France appears more similar to the *Wehrmacht*'s other great gamble, the attack on the Soviet Union in June 1941, than is commonly supposed. On both occasions, the *Wehrmacht* held no significant force in reserve. In both campaigns, the Germans gambled on achieving decisive success in the opening phase of the assault. Anything less spelled disaster. The very different outcomes are fully explicable in terms of conventional military logic. Against an opponent with a greater margin of material superiority, with better leadership and with more space in which to manoeuvre, the basic Napoleonic criterion for military success – superior force at the decisive point – would be far harder, if not impossible to achieve. Inspired soldiering could only do so much'.